Mass Appeal

Mass Appeal

The Depth and Beauty of the Eucharistic
Celebration at an Understandable Level

David DesOrmeaux

Writers Club Press
San Jose New York Lincoln Shanghai

Mass Appeal
The Depth and Beauty of the Eucharistic Celebration
at an Understandable Level

Writers Club Press
an imprint of iUniverse.com, Inc.

For information address:
iUniverse.com, Inc.
5220 S 16th, Ste. 200
Lincoln, NE 68512
www.iuniverse.com

ISBN: 0-595-19079-0

Printed in the United States of America

To Mom and Dad

CONTENTS

INTRODUCTION

The highest act of love the world has ever seen is Christ's offering of Himself to the Father for our salvation. That self-offering of Christ becomes present for us at every Mass.

Every Catholic has gone to Mass at least a few times. It's the one common experience all Catholics share. Yet many Catholics who have gone to Mass all their lives still don't understand it. Why is this? Well, it seems that by the time most cradle Catholics are old enough to understand the sacred words and actions of the Mass, it has become mere repetition. This causes many (or most) Catholics to say, "Mass is boring." These people no longer "get anything out of it" and ask, "Why do I have to go to Mass?" Teens, begging their parents to allow them to skip Mass, use pleas such as, "I'm going to sleep whether I'm at home or at Church, so why make me go?"

On several occasions when I was in my early teens, I realized after coming home from Mass that I hadn't said a word the entire time I was in church. I didn't sing; I didn't pray; I didn't respond to a single prayer. I suspect that I wasn't alone in my boredom. We see the same priest with the same flaws at the same altar saying the same prayers, and the repetition becomes too much to handle. So what should we do? How does one find meaning in the Mass and more importantly open the door to the veritable storehouse of grace waiting to be given to us?

If so many people are bored during Mass, there must be something wrong with it, right? We get excited about shopping. A $5,000 shopping spree would put a smile on almost any lady's face. We get excited about sports. Guys, how would you like a couple of tickets to the Superbowl? We get excited about many things, but Mass doesn't excite us. So there must be something wrong with it, right? We could change the Mass to make it more exciting. We could play upbeat songs and let everyone have a special job in the Mass. The focus could be on fellowship and fun. Although this plan has had some success in getting people interested, it has several drawbacks and I think that there is a better way. **We don't need to change the Mass; we need to be changed by the Mass!** We as Catholics are not seeing the Mass for what it is. Why?

As alluded to earlier, many Catholics who have been attending Mass all of their lives have only a child's understanding of the prayers and actions. It is not unusual to find men and women sitting in the pews each week who have Ph.D.'s in Business and a seven year old's comprehension of the Mass. I believe we Catholics will not be able to see how wonderful the Mass really is until we understand it better. For even miracles may not look impressive to us if we can't see them in the right way.

For instance, you can't see the aurora borealis if you are in Brazil.[1] Even though it is a beautiful miracle, these northern lights can only be seen if you are in the northern hemisphere. You must be in the right place physically. Similarly, you must be in the right place mentally in order to see how beautiful the miracle of the Mass is.

For sometimes even miracles—miracles as wondrous as the aurora borealis or the Mass—don't impress us because we don't look at them from the right viewpoint. **The miracle isn't what's lacking; our understanding of the miracle is lacking.** Mass seems long only because our love is short.

The Holy Mass is full of symbolism. Every action and phrase has a deeper meaning. "The theology of the liturgy is in a special way 'symbolic theology,' a theology of symbols, which connects us to what is present but hidden."[2] Symbols never express the fullness of the Eucharistic Mystery, but they do guide us toward these deep mysteries, bringing us closer to

---

1. The author realizes there is a similar phenomenon, the aurora australis, which may be seen in countries south of the equator, but is here referring to the northern lights in particular.
2. Ratzinger. *Spirit of the Liturgy*. Ignatius, p. 60.

God. As St. Bonaventure said, "The Holy Mass is as full of mysteries as the ocean is full of drops, or as the sky is full of stars, and as the courts of Heaven are full of angels." By unraveling some of these mysteries of the Mass, we will begin to find new significance in the Mass and receive lasting graces from it.

It's time to get excited about the Mass! The excitement that we need is not an empty emotional high that fades with time but the type of excitement that helps us to dive deeper and deeper into our love of Christ through the Mass.

Preparing For Mass

Most of our prayers have the same basic format. The goal is the Father, the way is the Son, the power is the Holy Spirit. The Mass follows this outline. It is a prayer to God the Father (Luke 11:2), through Jesus Christ his Son (1 Timothy 2:5), in the Holy Spirit (Revelation 1:10). We, the Church, join with Jesus in offering this beautiful prayer to the Father.

As we prepare for Mass, the first item to keep in mind is fasting. Before receiving the Eucharist, we fast for one hour out of respect for Jesus' Body and Blood. Prior to the Second Vatican Council, Catholics fasted all morning until receiving Communion at Mass. This fasting is related to the Jewish practice of fasting before the Passover meal each year. Although we have a much easier duty, only having to fast for an hour, our **fasting still makes us hunger and thirst for the Lord in the Eucharist.**

You're looking through your closet wondering what to wear to church, grab a pair of jeans, throw on that crumpled up tee-shirt that was under the bed and run off to Mass. Maybe I could suggest a different strategy. Don't wait to start getting dressed until ten minutes before Mass; leave yourself plenty of time to get ready. Also, think about where you are going so you'll **know what is appropriate to wear.** The way we dress for an event shows how important we think that event is. When an occasion is important to us we wear nice clothes. You wouldn't wear a tee-shirt and jeans to prom or to a wedding or a job interview, so don't wear those clothes to church. Mass should be the center of our lives. Wear your Sunday best.

We jump into the car, turn on the radio, drive across town to the church, park the car, and run up to the front doors of the church (and only 10 minutes late this Sunday). You are about to enter the sacred zone.

You're not entering just any old house. **This is God's house**. The church is a place set aside for Him so remember your focus should be on God.

In the early days of Christianity, many people kissed the ground as they entered a church, showing that it is a extraordinary place. I'm not implying you should drop down and kiss the ground every time you enter a church, but it is good to keep in mind what an awesome place the church is.

Immediately after going into the church most people spot those containers, called fonts, which hold holy water. We dip our fingers in the water and make the sign of the cross. What's up with that, you ask? The **holy water (John 3:5) and sign of the cross (Mt. 28:19) remind us of our Baptism**. So this holy water/sign of the cross action is a renewal of Baptism. Since the sacrament of Baptism brings us into the Church, the family of faith, this dipping in holy water reminds us that we are united in one Christian Baptism. This is a particularly good time to be reminded of our Baptism for at this moment we are physically entering the church to join the congregation, the family of faith. At Baptism, we spiritually entered the Church, joining the Family of God.

Now, after our holy water stop, we cruise down the aisle and see the girl in front of us kneel on one knee before going into the rows of pews. This kneeling on the right knee is called genuflection. In ancient times, citizens would genuflect to their king as a sign of adoration. **If our king, Jesus, is present in the church under the appearance of bread, we genuflect to Him** before finding our seat. If He is not present in the church, there is no need to genuflect but we should bow to the altar out of respect for that holy table of sacrifice where Jesus becomes present for us.

After finding a place to sit, we kneel down, this time on both knees, to pray. Kneeling on both knees is also a sign of adoration and humility (Matthew 17:14; Mark 1:40; 10:17). It should remind us of Jesus' posture (Luke 22:41) in the Garden of Gethsemane on the Mount of Olives, where in agony He prayed to his Father about his coming death.

Usually we make the sign of the cross and then fold our hands together. This action of holding our hands together may seem insignificant, but actually it is very important. When a person slides the fingers of one hand into the fingers of the other and grips them together (hands clasped), this action means, "I want my will to be bound with the will of God, just as one hand is strongly bound to the other." Therefore, we pray that our wants will be the same as what God wants. Further, this action represents the binding together of the people of God. Our fingers represent the people and they are joined strongly together when we fold our hands, just as we will be joined at Mass.

There is another way of holding your hands together that is commonly used and very significant. In this action your palms are placed flat against each other and all of your fingers point up symbolizing the prayer rising to Heaven. The heel or bottom of the hands are against the chest, showing that this prayer comes from your heart.

Now that we are kneeling, with our hands together, our bodies are ready to pray. But guess what isn't? Yeah, **our minds get distracted**. Troy is looking at Jessica and Jessica is trying to find Jennifer. Nobody is praying! No one has even said "hello" to God! We need to gather our composure. Close your eyes, be still, and empty your mind of all distractions. Collect yourself. This is God's time; concentrate on Him.

We come to worship the Lord but first we must find Him. You won't find Him by constantly talking to the person next to you or by looking around to see who is coming in the door. He will be found in the silence. Close your eyes and be still. As St. Ambrose said, "the devil wants noise, Christ wants stillness." **Christ will be found in the silence and stillness**.

But we fill our days with noise on purpose! Many Americans are talking to someone (in person or on the phone), watching television, or listening to the radio at all times. They are afraid of silence. But in order to listen to God, to know what He wants, we need some silence. To meditate on the prayers and scripture in Mass, we need some silence. Out of silence comes the virtues of reverence, humility, patience and respect for others. The greatest thoughts and deepest prayers are born in silence.

So now that our bodies are in position and our minds are ready for prayer, how do we pray? What if I can't think of anything to pray about? Obviously it is good to pray for personal intentions involving family, friends, and so on, but there are some other intentions to pray for before Mass begins.

First of all, pray for the priest who will be saying Mass. We may not know the particular priest who is going to celebrate the Mass until it begins, but we can make a general prayer for priests. They all need our prayers. They are overworked and underPRAYED. Our priests have devoted their lives to God by serving us, so the least we can do is pray for them. Pray that they have patience with us, strength to carry on, and zeal for God's work. They need prayers just like we do.

The second thing to pray about is your spiritual life. Review the day(s) since you last went to Mass. What have you done that is spiritually good? Have you been praying more? Reading the Bible more? Tolerating your irritating little brother? Not complaining even though you're in pain? Not getting upset when your spouse or parents nag you? These good things will be used later in the Mass so keep them in mind. What have you done that is spiritually bad? What sins have you committed? If you have sinned mortally since your last confession (Reconciliation) then remember that you can't receive Communion at this Mass. What small sins have you committed? Also keep these in your mind since they will be addressed in Mass very soon.

Okay, we've got the pre-Mass prayer down, so what's next on the list? I would recommend looking over the readings before Mass begins. Also, get ready to participate. We don't come to church as a spectator. Our participation in the holy Mass is our worship of God. We should be active by responding to the prayers, singing (I know, I don't sing very well either, but try!), and listening. You won't enjoy the Mass until you put forth some effort. The fruits of the Mass, that is, the grace you receive from it, depend on how you participate.

Introductory Rites

The introductory rites help the faithful come together to form a community and prepares them to listen to God's word and to celebrate the Eucharist.

Following is a general outline of the Mass on the Feast of the Body and Blood of Christ. The Mass you attend on any given Sunday will have similarities to and differences from this one. Those prayers and actions of the Mass which are part of every Mass are called "the ordinary." Those prayers used only on that particular day of the liturgical year are called "the proper." This book focuses mainly on Sunday Mass, so if you are one of the faithful who go to Mass during the week, you will see some differences. The actual words used in Mass are in italics while my comments are in normal type. As you read the words used in Mass, notice the Bible references that are provided for almost every phrase of the Mass. Most people are surprised at how much of the Mass is from Sacred Scripture.[3]

Entrance Procession

Someone who had never been to a Mass would immediately be surprised as the altar servers, ministers and priest walk up the center aisle. What are all those weird clothes that the priest is wearing and why is he wearing them?

The **alb** (Exodus 28; Revelation 7:13-14; Leviticus 16:4) is a full length white linen robe that has come to symbolize the purity of soul that comes

---

3. The Scripture references included in the text of the Mass come primarily from the work of Fr. Peter Stravinskas.

to us in Baptism and with which the Mass should be offered. It is the garment Christ was clothed in by Herod (Luke 23:11) and is common to ministers of every rank.

The **cincture** is the rope belt tied around the waist of the alb. It has come to symbolize chastity and the cord that Christ was bound with when He was arrested in the Garden on the Mount of Olives. Further, it represents the binding of the priest to the will of God and to his superiors.

The **stole** is a long, narrow strip of cloth which hangs from the priest's neck down in front of his chest on each side. It has come to symbolize the light burden of Christ (Matthew 11:28-30) and the dignity of the priesthood. It is a sign that the priest is performing his priestly work and has authority to preach and administer the sacraments.

The **chasuble** is a sleeveless garment worn over all the other vestments. It is often decorated with beautiful symbols and is in the color of the feast day or liturgical season. Because the chasuble is basically a big circle of cloth with an opening in the center for the priest's head, it looks like a poncho or shawl. The word "chasuble" comes from the Latin word "casula" meaning "little house" since it covers the priest and all his other garments. It is worn on the outside because it symbolizes the love which priests must put on above all else. Also, this garment reminds us of the purple robe the soldier clothed Jesus with at the crowning with thorns (Mark 15:17 and John 19:2).

In addition to these garments, a bishop will also have a miter (Exodus 28, Leviticus 16:4) and crosier when he presides over Mass. The **miter** is a two pointed (front and back) hat symbolic of union of the Old and New Testaments. Under the miter the bishop wears a small skull cap called a zucchetto. A bishop's zucchetto is purple and the pope's is white.

The **crosier** or shepherd's staff shows that the bishop shepherds Christ's flock. It is also related to Aaron's rod that budded (symbolizing priesthood) and the staves the twelve Apostles (our first bishops) took on one of the their missions (Mark 6:8).

While the priest celebrates Mass, he stands "in persona Christi," meaning, in the person of Christ. In the entrance procession we can see the priest acting as Christ did on the way to his death. Before the Middle Ages, it was customary in some regions for a priest to carry the cross in the entrance procession up to the altar. This action paralleled Jesus carrying his cross.

The side walls of our churches are often lined with the stations of the cross. These tell of Jesus' journey to the cross and of his crucifixion. So as the priest, standing in persona Christi, walks down the aisle lined with the stations of the cross, he looks like Jesus on the way of the cross. Then as the priest walks up onto the altar platform, we can imagine Christ walking up Calvary hill towards his death. Finally, the priest's journey is finished when he reaches the place traditionally associated with sacrifice, the altar. Likewise, Jesus' journey ends when He is sacrificed for our sins on the cross. Consequently, our altar represents the cross and the cross is the altar of the New Covenant. In this way the entrance procession symbolizes Christ's way to the cross.

Veneration of the Altar

When they arrive at the altar, the priest, altar servers, and whoever else is in the procession give proper reverence. If the Blessed Sacrament is present in the sanctuary area, the proper reverence is a genuflection. If He is not present, a profound (bending at the waist) bow is appropriate.[4]

As a sign of veneration, the priest **kisses the altar**, or more specifically, the relic in the altar. The relic is usually a bone of a saint or a splinter of wood from Christ's cross. The splinter of wood again points out the connection between Christ's cross and our altar. Also, the altar has always been associated with martyrs (martyrs are people who die for the faith. See

---

4. *General Instruction of the Roman Missal (2000)*, nos. 49, 274.

Revelation 6:9). Just as Christ sacrificed his own life for us on the cross which is represented by the altar, the martyrs were sacrificed for Christ and buried in rock tombs. In the early Church, therefore, Mass was celebrated in the catacombs on the tombs of martyrs. These tombs were the altars of the early church. As the priest celebrated Mass on a tomb, he would ask for intercessory prayer from the saint whose bones were in that tomb. This practice continues through the use of relics in altars. A larger example of this is St. Peter's tomb below the altar in St. Peter's Basilica in Rome.

Incensing (Leviticus 16:12; Psalm 141:2) the altar may also be appropriate at this time as a sign of reverence and purification. **Incense** can be used "during the entrance procession; at the beginning of Mass, to incense the cross and the altar; at the procession and proclamation of the gospel reading;" at the preparation of the gifts; and after the consecration.[5] After being spooned from an incense boat, the incense is burned in a device called a censer or a thurible. The rising smoke of incense symbolizes the prayers of the saints (cf. Rev 5:8).

The altar is also the center piece in the central action (the Mass) of the life of the Church. The Mass is the center of the Church's life because every Catholic takes part in this grace-filled celebration. The altar is the center piece of the celebration because Christ becomes present there. Thus the Catechism calls the altar "the center of the church."[6] In this way **the altar symbolizes the very heart of the Church.**

Consequently the priest, standing in the person of Christ, shows the union of Christ and his Bride, the Church (Ephesians 5:21-32) through the action of kissing her heart, the altar. We can see clearly **through Christ kissing his Bride that the Mass we are about to take part in is nothing less than the Marriage Supper of the Lamb.**

---

5. *General Instruction of the Roman Missal (2000)*, no. 276.
6. *Catechism of the Catholic Church*, par. 1182.

The altar is also the threshold between Heaven and earth. As the Mass unfolds, watch closely as the gap between the perfect Heavenly Liturgy and our lowly Eucharistic Liturgy is bridged on the altar right in front of our eyes. **Christ brings us, his Bride, into a foretaste of Heaven through the actions on the sacred altar at Mass.** This is not just a metaphor; we join with the choirs of angels in singing praise to God and partake of the sacrifice of Christ on the cross.

But we can't let anyone know about this. ☺ We have to keep it secret. If word gets out about this, that is, if people find out how wondrous Mass really is, we will never be able to get a seat in the church! Not only will the place be packed hours before, but people will camp outside the doors of the church days ahead of time just to get a seat in the church!

Let's get the word out about the Mass! We need to let everyone know, Catholic and non-Catholic alike, how awesome the Mass really is.

Sign of the Cross

Priest: In the name of the Father, and of the Son, and of the Holy Spirit (Matthew 28:19).
All: Amen (1 Chronicles 16:36).

As we make the sign of the cross, it reminds the Lord of his sufferings and shows Him the Church, his Bride, is remembering that He died for her sake.

In the early Church, the sign of cross was traced on the forehead (Revelation 14:1; 7:3), not the whole upper body as we do today. Slaves of that day were marked on their foreheads to indicate who their owner or master was, and similarly, Christians traced the sign of the cross on their forehead to designate themselves as slaves of God. He is our Master. But instead of taking away our freedom, God our true Master gives us the ultimate freedom, eternal life.

Later it became common to make the sign of the cross on the head, chest and shoulders as we do now. The forehead is marked because it is the place of understanding, the chest because feelings come from the heart, and the shoulders because the arms work to bear fruit. Accordingly Jesus Christ should be in our every thought, driving all our emotions, and the goal of all our labor. We pray that God will give us the mind to know Him, the heart to love Him, and the strength to serve Him.

The Sign of the cross is a summary of the whole Christian faith. By mentioning the Father, Son and Holy Spirit, the sign of the cross refers to the deepest mystery of Christianity, the Trinity (three Persons in one God). Understandably, the sign of the cross also reminds us of the crucifixion and as such is the very symbol of Christ's death. But the cross can never be viewed alone, it always must be seen in light of what it accomplished, namely, the redemption of the whole human race. Because we know what Christ's death accomplished, the sign of the cross is also the symbol of new life. Jesus' death in the crucifixion and rising to new life in the Resurrection provide a model for our dying to self through repentance and rising to new life in Him through Baptism. For in Baptism, we for the first time receive the grace that Christ won for us on the cross.

The link between Baptism and the sign of the cross can likewise be observed as Jesus instructs his Apostles to "make disciples of all nations, baptizing them in the name of the Father, and of the Son, and of the Holy Spirit" (Matthew 28:19). Therefore the sign of the cross relates the basics of the faith: the Trinity, redemption and Baptism.

Greeting of the Congregation

Priest: The grace and peace of the Lord Jesus Christ and the love of God and the fellowship of the Holy Spirit be with you all (2 Corinthians 13:13).
All: And also with you (Ruth 2:4).

The greeting officially begins the sacred liturgy (liturgy means public ceremonial worship). The priest's comments here are **the Christian version of hello and good morning**. But the greeting given in Mass is far superior to an ordinary hello. Listen to what the priest is praying upon us: the peace, love, and fellowship of God Himself. Even more, the priest wishes grace upon us. What exactly is grace, you ask? It is God's own eternal life, won for us on the cross by Jesus and given to us as a free, undeserved gift, enabling us to live a holy life on earth and be with Him in Heaven. What an awesome greeting!

It is easy to fall into the mindset that we should be entertained during Mass. When you go to the movies, sitting in rows of seats with a bunch of other people, you are the audience. When you go watch a football game and sit in rows of seats with a crowd of other people around you, you are the audience. As we begin the holy Celebration of the Eucharist, we sit in pews with a group of people around us, but realize that **we are NOT the audience in the Mass**. The purpose of Mass is not for us to be entertained. We, along with the priest, are participants in the Holy Mass. God the Father is the "audience," so to speak. The Mass is a prayer of Christ and the Church, that is, us, to the Father by the power of the Holy Spirit. We, as the congregation, are at Mass to offer worship by praying and singing and offering our own lives to God.

Penitential Rite (Confiteor)

All: I confess to almighty God, and to you, my brothers and sisters, that I have sinned through my own fault (James 5:16) in my thoughts and in my words (James 3:6), in what I have done, and in what I have failed to do (James 4:17); and I ask Blessed Mary, ever virgin, all the angels and saints, and you, my brothers and sisters, to pray for me to the Lord our God (1 Thessalonians 5:25; 1 Timothy 2:1).

Priest: May almighty God have mercy on us, forgive us our sins, and bring us to everlasting life (1 John 1:9).
(Many make the sign of the cross)
All: Amen (1 Chronicles 16:36).

Remember before Mass when you prayed about the sins you committed since your last Mass? Here in the Penitential Rite, the small ones can be forgiven. An examination of conscience should be made before Mass since enough time may not be available at this juncture of our Eucharistic Celebration. Recognizing that we have sinned (1 John 1:8), we publicly (along with the priest) confess our sins (James 5:16) so that our Eucharistic sacrifice may be pure (Didache 14). If we ignore our sinfulness and receive the most holy Eucharist in an unworthy manner, we "will have to answer for the Body and Blood of the Lord" (1 Corinthians 11:27).

Why, you ask, do we request the prayers from the Lord's holy Mother Mary, the angels, the saints, and each other? This is done because we want the entire Family of God, the Church, to beg the Lord God to forgive us. Additionally, we want their continued prayers so that we won't fall into sin again. Not only do we ask for the prayers of the saints, we also request "you, my brothers and sisters, to pray for me to the Lord our God."

Do you take this seriously? Do you pray for these people are in need of your prayers? Please pray for me!

After we the faithful make a "general confession" ("I confess to Almighty God...."), the Penitential Rite is "concluded with the priest's absolution"[7] as he bestows God's forgiveness on us. Some people make the sign of the cross at this time just like when the words of absolution are given to us in the confessional. This **mini-confession** that the faithful make, though it is not a Sacrament and "lacks the efficacy of the sacrament of penance,"[8] can rid us of venial sin if used correctly. Mortal sins, however,

---

7. *General Instruction of the Roman Missal (2000)*, no. 51.
8. Ibid.

need the more serious repentance of the Sacrament of Reconciliation (also called Confession or Penance).

Here in the Penitential Rite the worshiper uses "I" instead of "we." This is because I need to look inside my own heart and see the sinfulness. No one else can do that but me. It is important to realize that I am ultimately responsible for what I do. I can't say, "the devil made me do it!" No, mea culpa, it's my fault. After we are made pure in this rite, the worshiper is entitled to act and speak as part of the "we" that is the Church.

Kyrie (Greek "Kyrie Eleison" means "Lord have mercy")

Priest: Lord have mercy (Tobit 8:4). All: Lord have mercy (Ps 30:11).
Priest: Christ have mercy (Luke 18:38). All: Christ have mercy (Mk 10:46, 1 Tim 1:2). Priest: Lord have mercy (Ps 51:1-3). All: Lord have mercy (Ps 6:2).

Although the three part structure of the Kyrie may appear to be Trinitarian, the Kyrie has historically been a litany to Jesus alone. Each of the three times mercy is requested, some in the congregation lightly strike their chests, reminiscent of the tax collector in Luke 18:13. In the fourth century St. Augustine of Hippo had to caution his people because, strangely enough, some of them were injuring themselves during the Kyrie by beating their chests too hard! We need to have that kind of sorrow for our sins, but in a **spiritual** rather than **physical** manner.

We, the Church, have confessed our sinfulness and begged for God's mercy. The Lord has heard us and forgiven our sins. By this point, our souls are properly prepared through purification to precede past the penitential portion of the Mass to participation in the principal parts. Christ is perfect and pure Himself, so nothing less than the best bride will do. Now we, the Church, are ready to be Christ's pure Bride. We are prepared for what lies ahead—the Wedding Supper of the Lamb.

Gloria (Glory to God)

All: Glory to God in the highest, and peace to His people on earth (Luke 2:14). Lord God, heavenly King, almighty God and Father (Revelation 19:6), we worship you (Revelation 22:9), we give you thanks (Ephesians 5:20), we praise you for your glory (Revelation 7:12). Lord Jesus Christ, only Son of the Father (2 John v. 3), Lord God, Lamb of God (Revelation 5:6) you take away the sin of the world (John 1:29): have mercy on us (Matthew 15:22); You are seated at the right hand of the Father (1 Peter 3:22; Acts 7:55-56), receive our prayer (Romans 8:34). For you alone are the Holy One (Luke 4:34), you alone are the Lord (Revelation 15:4), you alone are the most high (Psalm 83:19, Luke 1:32), Jesus Christ, with the Holy Spirit and the glory of God the Father (John 14:26). Amen.

This one powerful prayer contains all four of the main types of prayer:
- Adoration or Praise: "We worship you…, we praise you…"
- Thanksgiving: "We give you thanks…for your glory."
- Contrition for sins: "You take away the sin of the world: have mercy on us."
- Supplication or Petition: "Receive our prayer."

The Lord has just forgiven us, it is time to shout with joy! **The Gloria is our joyous exclamation.** God has taken an old, ugly woman scarred by sin and turned her into the most beautiful, pure, sinless virgin Bride. He has sanctified the Church, "cleansing her by the bath of water with the word. That he might present to himself the church in splendor, without spot or wrinkle or any such thing, that she might be holy and without blemish" (Ephesians 5:26).

In the Gloria we thank God for allowing us to be counted as worthy to receive his Body and Blood, his own self-offering.

Opening Prayer

Priest: Lord Jesus Christ, You gave us the Eucharist as the memorial of your suffering and death. May our worship of this sacrament of your Body and Blood help us to experience the salvation You won for us and the peace of the kingdom where you live with the Father and the Holy Spirit, one God, for ever and ever. All: Amen.

The priest prays the opening prayer in the orans position. The orans position consists of open hands held out from the shoulders and raised about neck high. The position helps us to imagine our prayer flowing toward God above. Our open hands symbolize peace since open hands can't hold weapons. Because the orans position imitates Christ's position on the cross, our Father may look down on our prayer and remember his Son Jesus' self-offering.

The Opening Prayer is also called the Collect because it sums up and gathers together all the intentions of the day's sacrifice. It often clues us in to whose feast day it is or what liturgical season is being celebrated. Another good clue as to what feast of season is being celebrated is the **colors** used in the church. The clothing of the priest, the cloths which hang down in front of the altar (called antependium cloths, not to be confused with the white altar cloths which symbolize Christ's burial cloths cf. John 19:40.) and the banners or tapestries in the church indicate to the congregation what liturgical season is being celebrated.

White is used during joyful or glorious commemorations of Jesus' life such as Christmas or Easter. It may also be used for feasts of the Virgin Mary, angels, or non-martyred saints to show purity. The color red as the color of blood is used on the feast days of martyrs. Martyrs, you will recall, are people who are killed because they refuse to give up the faith. For this same reason red is also used on all feasts dealing with our Lord's cross and Passion, and the feasts of the Apostles. To symbolize the fire of the Holy Spirit (Acts 2:3), red is used at Pentecost and for Masses of the Holy Spirit.

Purple is a symbol of penance and expiation. It is used during Advent and Lent. Green is the color of growing vegetation and hope. It is used during ordinary time to remind us that even in ordinary times we should always be growing closer and closer to the Lord. Other colors are used on special occasions.

THE LITURGY OF THE WORD

"Man doesn't live on bread alone but on every word that comes from the mouth of God" (Deuteronomy 8:3; Amos 8:11; Luke 4:4; Matthew 4:4).

The Liturgy of the Word is the first of the two main parts of the Mass (caution: when the word "Liturgy" is used by itself, it is often being used to mean "Mass"). The second of the two parts is the Liturgy of the Eucharist. In the Liturgy of the Word, the Sacred Scriptures are proclaimed to us so we may come to know God and his mission for us. The Second Vatican Council requested that "The treasures of the Bible…be opened up more lavishly so that a richer fare may be provided for the faithful at the table of God's word."[9] Consequently we have, since the Council, added another reading to the Liturgy of the Word. The Church urges us to read the Bible more frequently since "…sacred Scripture [is] the abiding source of spiritual life, the foundation for Christian instruction, and the core of all theological study."[10] We are also reminded by Holy Mother Church that,

> "Although the sacred liturgy is principally the worship of the divine majesty it likewise contains much instruction for the faithful. For in the Liturgy God speaks to his people, and Christ is still proclaiming his Gospel. And the people reply to God both by song and prayer."[11]

---

9. *Constitution on the Sacred Liturgy*, art. 51.
10. Paul VI. Apostolic Constitution, Promulgation of the Roman Missal.
11. *Constitution on the Sacred Liturgy*, art. 33.

In essence, this indicates that God is teaching his people about Himself through the Mass. This takes place especially in the readings and accompanying explanation in the Liturgy of the Word. For "[w]hen the Scriptures are read in the Church, God himself is speaking to his people, and Christ, present in his own word, is proclaiming the gospel."[12]

The Liturgy of the Word imitates the action of God Himself. In the history of the world it has always been God who initiates communication with humanity. He reveals Himself to them and calls them to come home to the Father through the Son by the power of the Holy Spirit. The word of God which we hear in the Liturgy of the Word does the same thing, calling out to us to hear God's message, pray about it, and respond to it. It calls us into the universal Family of God. So the Liturgy of the Word is a reflection of God's own divine dealings with humanity.

First Reading: Genesis 14:18-20

Reader: A reading from the book of Genesis.
Melchizedek, king of Salem, brought out bread and wine, and being a priest of God Most High, he blessed Abram with these words: "Blessed be Abram by God Most High, the Creator of heaven and earth; And blessed be God Most High, who delivered your foes into your hand."
Reader: The word of the Lord.
All: Thanks be to God.

It is not mere coincidence that we sit to listen to lectures in school and we also sit to hear the first two readings. Sitting is a very good posture for careful listening and learning. Read from the Lectionary on the lectern (also called the ambo or pulpit), the Scripture readings are ways in which God speaks to his people, teaching us the mysteries of redemption and salvation. The Sunday readings follow a three year cycle: year A is the Gospel

---

12. *General Instruction of the Roman Missal (2000)*, no. 29.

of Matthew, year B is Mark, and year C is Luke. John's Gospel is used during parts of Lent, the Easter season, and because Mark's Gospel is short, also during year B.

The **first reading usually comes to us from the Old Testament** (except during Easter season). These Old Testament readings show us how the old covenant leads into and is fulfilled by the New Covenant.

Old Testament Background of the Mass

There are certain events in the Old Testament which strongly resemble Christ's eternal sacrifice that is re-presented in the Mass or resemble certain symbols and prayers that we use in the Mass. We say these Old Testament events prefigure the Mass, meaning that they are a figure or type of the Mass that came before the first Mass, the Last Supper. Another related term is **typology**, the study of those Old Testament figures and their fulfillment in the time of Christ and his Church. After learning some basic information about sacrifice, we'll look at some of these Old Testament types to see how they relate to the Mass.

The word "**sacrifice**" means to make something sacred, to set it aside and make it holy for God. The basic idea behind it is to give back to God what rightly belongs to Him. Sacrifice is at the center of worship for all religions. Since the Fall of humanity in the Garden of Eden, sacrifice has involved destroying the item being offered. The physical destruction of the thing being offered, the victim, gives that victim back to God spiritually. The central action of a sacrifice is not the slaughter but the offering of the victim to God.

Sacrifice of Abel Genesis 4:1-4:12

Also see Hebrews 11:4

We have sacrificed from the very beginning. It is in our (fallen) nature. This is evident in the account of Cain and Abel. Sons of Adam and Eve,

Cain was a farmer and Abel was a shepherd. They both offered sacrifice to God but Abel gave his best sheep to the Lord, while Cain didn't bring his best produce. God was excited about Abel's offering and Cain became envious. Cain's jealousy of Abel's favor with the Lord led to him murdering the innocent Abel.

Now that you are familiar with the basics of the story, let's look at how Abel and his sacrifice parallels Jesus and his sacrifice which is made present at the Mass.

Abel	*Jesus*
was a shepherd (keeper of flocks)	is the Good Shepherd (John 10:11)
offers the best lamb to God in sacrifice	offers Himself, the perfect Lamb of God (John 1:36), to the Father in sacrifice
Jewish tradition says Abel was not married (celibate)	Jesus was not married
offers animal sacrifice, so he is a priest	He is the high priest (Hebrews 8:1)
God looks with favor on Abel and his offering	The Father looks with favor on Jesus and his self-offering
Abel's father was Adam. The word "Adam" is the same word as "man" in Hebrew. So Abel is the son of "man."	Jesus often called Himself the Son of Man (Matthew 19:28 for example).
was killed for his love of God, the first martyr of the Old Covenant	Was killed for his love of God, the first martyr of the New Covenant

Sacrifice of Noah Genesis 8:20-21

We're all familiar with the story of Noah and the flood. The world was corrupt and God asked Noah to build an ark and pack all kinds of animals on it. The flood came and Noah floated his way to a new life. That is where the story ends for most people. But there is more. Let's take a look at, as Paul Harvey might say, the rest of the story. Immediately after Noah steps off the ark, he built an altar and offered animals and birds as holocausts to the Lord. Noah offered sacrifice which by definition makes him a priest. God smelled the smoke of the holocaust sacrifice and promised not to condemn all the earth again. Our present day priests (acting in the person of Christ) use an altar and offer the one truly pure sacrifice: Jesus Christ. The Father smells the sweet smell of his Son's self-sacrifice and swears that humanity will never be doomed again. He promises we will have a chance to receive eternal life in Heaven.

Offering of Melchizedek Genesis 14:18-20

Also see Psalm 110:4; Hebrews 5:6-10; Hebrews 6:20; 7:1-21

While you have probably heard of Abel and Noah, Melchizedek (sometimes spelled Melchisedech) is a new name to many Catholics. He is a priest/king who offered bread and wine as a sacrifice to God. The offering of Melchizedek images the Mass, at which bread and wine become the Body and Blood of Christ. Melchizedek also images Christ in many ways. Look at the relation between Melchizedek and Christ:

Melchizedek	*Jesus*
His name means "righteous king" (Hebrew 7:1)	is our righteous king
King of Salem (meaning peace) which later became Jerusalem	King of Kings and prince of peace, ruling over the New Jerusalem
Priest of God Most High	Most High Priest of God
Bestows blessings on Abram (Abraham)	Gives blessings to all
Offered bread and wine in the sacrifice	Offered consecrated bread and wine (His Body and Blood) in the Last Supper sacrifice

Sacrifice of Isaac Genesis 22:1-18

Also see Hebrews 11:17-19; Romans 8:31

God promised to make Abraham the father of more people than he could count. But Abraham was too old to father any children. So God worked a miracle and Abraham fathered Isaac. If we fast forward a few years we see God asking Abraham to sacrifice Isaac. Thank goodness Abraham was a man of tremendous faith. He did what God asked, preparing what was needed to sacrifice Isaac. Abraham took his knife and was about to slaughter Isaac when God sent a messenger to stop him. Abraham looked up and there was a ram to take Isaac's place as the sacrifice. God is good to those who are faithful to Him! All Jewish people since that time point to Abraham as their father. Father Abraham seems to have much in common with God our Father. And so after looking at this Bible passage, what similarities can we find between Abraham and God?

Father Abraham	*God the Father*
known for his faithfulness	known for his faithfulness
had one precious beloved son, Isaac[13]	has one precious beloved Son, Jesus
willing to offer up his only son	willing to offer up his only Son (Romans 8:32; John 3:16)
becomes father of a countless many	becomes Father of countless many

Interestingly enough, Isaac in many ways resembles Christ. For instance, a Jewish writing from the second century before Christ asserts that Isaac was offered up in the same month on the same day at the very hour the paschal lamb would be sacrificed in the Temple. According to John's Gospel on the other hand, Jesus was also offered up on the same month, day, and hour as the paschal lamb was slaughtered in the Temple. What other similarities can we see between Isaac and Jesus?

---

13. The author realizes that Abraham fathered a son, Ishmael, with his maid-servant Hagar. However, Isaac is Abraham's one true son with Sarah his wife. Similarly, Jesus is God the Father's only true beloved Son by nature, yet we are adopted children of God.

Isaac	*Jesus*
only son of father	only Son of Father
rode to place of his sacrifice on donkey	rode to place of his sacrifice, Jerusalem, on either donkey or colt (Matthew 21:2)
carried the wood on which he would be sacrificed	carried the wood cross on which he would be sacrificed
knife to pierce him	nails and lance pierce him
God provided a ram for the sacrifice so Isaac didn't have to die	God provide the Lamb of God who suffered so we don't have to spiritually die in hell
bound and put on wood	bound, then put on cross
sentenced to die but "returned from death"	sentenced to die, was killed, then resurrected from death

Jewish Passover Meal Exodus 12

Also see Deuteronomy 26:5-8

The Last Supper, which was the first Eucharistic Celebration (Mass), took place within the context of a Jewish Passover meal. By taking a closer look at the historical events of the Passover and the Passover meal, we should be able to better understand Jesus' actions at the Last Supper and what significance they hold regarding the Mass.

The book of Exodus tells of Moses and his brother Aaron being commanded by God to go to the Pharaoh of Egypt and tell him to let the enslaved Israelites, God's chosen people, go free. Pharaoh stubbornly refused to let the Israelites go so the Lord sent ten plagues down upon the Egyptians. The tenth (and worst) plague was the death of every firstborn boy.

In order for the Israelites themselves to avoid being subjected to this plague, God gave them specific instructions on how to sidestep this catastrophe. Every family took a one year old male lamb without blemish and slaughtered it. The family applied the blood to the door frame and then roasted and ate the flesh. In addition they were to eat this meal dressed and ready for travel since, after all the Egyptian firstborns were killed, Pharaoh would drive the Israelites out of Egypt.

The Israelites followed these commands and everything happened exactly like the Lord had said. Death passed over Egypt and killed the firstborn son in every home that didn't follow the rules God had set forth. The Israelites were then delivered out of Egypt (via the parting of the Red Sea).

One final command was given to the Israelites regarding this Passover: the Passover meal was to be celebrated every year to commemorate their deliverance from slavery. God said, "This day shall be a memorial feast for you, which all your generations shall celebrate with pilgrimages to the Lord, as a perpetual institution…you must eat unleavened bread…Keep then this custom of the unleavened bread…you must celebrate this day throughout your generations as a perpetual institution" (Exodus 12:14-20). This yearly Passover feast commanded by the Lord renewed and strengthened the covenant bond between God and the Israelites.

Although there has been some change in the structure of the Passover meal, the following format was the one most likely followed by Jewish people when Jesus was alive.

Structure of Passover Seder meal:
1. The leader begins the meal with prayer of thanksgiving.
2. Festival blessing (kiddush) over first cup of wine (which was always mixed with water) then consumed along with bitter herbs.
3. Unleavened bread blest and consumed along with dipping sauce.
4. Read Passover account from scripture (Exodus 12:26; 13:8) and sings the little Hallel (Psalm 113), then blesses second cup of wine and consumed (cup of the haggadah).

5. Purification rite (ablution).
6. Blessing by father or leader over the bread.
7. Roasted Passover lamb eaten (main meal) along with unleavened bread.
8. Third cup of wine, the "cup of blessing" (1 Corinthians 10:16) is blessed and consumed.
9. The Great Hallel (Psalms 114-118) sung in praise of God.
10. The fourth cup of wine blessed and consumed (cup of culmination).

The Passover meal was the most important Jewish meal. The Jews saw it not only as a commemoration of the past events but as a present participation in the real events. As the Catechism states,

> "This is how Israel understands its liberation from Egypt: every time Passover is celebrated, the Exodus events are made present to the memory of believers so that they may conform their lives to them."[14]

This is the same view that we have of the Mass. It commemorates the Last Supper and Christ's Passion, Death, and Resurrection, but it also mysteriously makes those events present to us now.

This very significant concept must be understood, so let me repeat it in another way. Just as the Passover meal made the historical Passover and Exodus present years after the historical events were long gone, the Mass makes the Last Supper and Paschal Mystery present to us today. Again, when the Christian Passover, the Mass, is celebrated, Jesus' Exodus in Jerusalem (Luke 9:31), that is his Passion, Death, Resurrection and Ascension, become present here and now to us in a real yet mysterious way. This is not just my idea. The Catechism says the "**Christian liturgy not only recalls the events that saved us but actualizes them, makes them present.**"[15] Keep all of this in mind as we look at the Last Supper and the Mass.

---

14. *Catechism of the Catholic Church*, par. 1363.
15. Catechism of the Catholic Church, par. 1104.

The central act of the Passover was the offering and eating of the lamb. Similarly, the central act of our Mass is the offering and eating of the Lamb of God, Jesus. The Passover meal re-presented the basic events of the Israelites' salvation from Egyptian slavery and pagan idolatry. In a similar way, the new Passover, the Mass, re-presents the basic events of Christian salvation at the Passion, Death and Resurrection of Christ. Stated another way, while the historical Passover and Exodus freed God's people of the Old Testament from slavery in Egypt, the Last Supper and Paschal Mystery free God's People of the New Covenant from slavery to sin and death. Freedom from Egyptian slavery brought "new life" and so the historical Passover events became a symbol of creation and springtime. Likewise, Christ's Passover, the Mass, is an efficacious symbol of the new creation and eternal springtime.

Manna Exodus 16

Also see Numbers 11, Deuteronomy 8, Joshua 5, Nehemiah 9:20, Psalm 78:24-25; Wisdom 16:2-26; John 6; Revelation 2:17

After the Passover and Exodus out of Egyptian slavery, the Israelites were in the desert. They were hungry and it didn't take long for them to begin complaining about Moses and his brother Aaron bringing them into the desert. So God sent bread, called manna, that fell from the heavens every morning of the week except the Sabbath. The Israelites gathered and ate the manna everyday except for on the Sabbath when there was no manna to gather. On the day before the Sabbath, twice as much manna fell and was gathered so they would have enough to eat while resting on the Sabbath day. The Israelites always had enough to eat but never any extra (except the double portion on the day before the Sabbath). In this way God fed his people daily and they relied on Him for their most basic needs.

Manna relates to the word of God which fed the Israelites. "For man should not live on bread alone but on every word that flows from the mouth of God" (Dueteronomy 8:3; Luke 4:4, Matthew 4:4, Amos 8:11).

Manna is also a type of the Eternal Word of God (John 1:14), Jesus, present in the Eucharist. Of course the manna also looks like the altar bread that we use in Mass, but there is more to this comparison.

Many Jewish writings said the Messiah would bring down manna again during the Passover month. If we look into John chapter 6 (which will be described in more detail later), we see the crowd in effect saying to Jesus, "if you are the Messiah, then give us the expected Manna." Then Jesus shows them that He is the new Manna, the true Bread from Heaven (6:32), that will not only sustain their life temporarily like regular food but will bring them eternal life. This promised Bread of life (6:35), Jesus, was given to them during the month of the Passover at the Last Supper (which we know was a Passover meal).

To wrap up this section, I'll leave you with a question to think about. What is the "hidden manna" mentioned in Revelation 2:17?

Covenant Sacrifice, Meal, Proclamation Exodus 24

Remember when you were a little kid and you became "blood brothers" with your best friend? You liked your friend so much that you wanted to be closer than friends, you wanted to be family. Brotherhood, that is, a family bond, was created by mixing together a little blood from you and a little from your best friend. Love is often thicker than blood. When naturally unrelated people bond themselves together, making themselves into family, we call this arrangement a covenant. Following this definition, it is easy to see why Marriage is a covenant.

In his efforts to draw all people to Himself, God makes covenants with his people so we can all be part of the Family of God. In the Old Testament times these covenants (sacred family bonds) were sealed with the blood of animals, which showed a family (blood) relation between the people involved. Our New Covenant was sealed by the Blood of God Himself, Jesus Christ (Hebrews 9:12-22), and brings us together as the universal Family of God, the Catholic (which means "universal") Church.

Now let's apply this concept of covenant to Exodus 24:1-11. Moses as mediator of a covenant takes the blood of sacrificed animals, puts some of it on the altar, and then sprinkles the Israelites with the rest of it. What does this mean? The altar stands for God since the Israelites come into the closest union with Him through sacrifice on the altar. Blood represents life (Leviticus 17:14). So splashing blood on the Father (represented by the altar) and on people means they share the same blood, the same life. Furthermore, union with blood brings kinship. So this splashing of blood on God (the altar) and his people unites them in a sacred family bond, a covenant. The Israelites are being joined to the Father! They are God's family!

God seals the covenant and shows his love for his people by having a meal with them (vs. 11). Eating a meal with someone showed deep friendship and consequently this meal helped to bind the Father to his people. So who was included in this bond? Who was part of God's family after that covenant was formed? The altar that Moses makes has twelve pillars representing the twelve tribes of Israel. This shows that all of the Israelites are included in the covenant.

In basic items and actions this passage in Exodus 24 seems related to the Mass. We see an altar (vs. 4) with young priests (5) sacrificing (5) and a communion meal (11). The book of the covenant, God's word to the Israelites (7) is read to the people and they respond in one voice, professing their faith in his word (7).

After their "profession of faith" when the Israelites pledge to do everything God asks of them, they receive the blood of the covenant (8). In the Last Supper (Matthew 26:28), Jesus quotes this verse, Exodus 24:8, saying, "this is my blood of the covenant." Why is this significant? In Mass, we make a profession of faith (the Creed) before receiving the Blood of the New Covenant, Jesus' own Blood. So in this New Universal (that is, catholic) Covenant in Jesus' Blood, guess who becomes God's family?

Sacrifice Leviticus 1-7

The ancient sacrifices in the Book of Leviticus were only shadows of the true sacrifice to come. Each of them found their fulfillment in Christ's eternal sacrifice present historically on the cross and sacramentally in the Mass. Let's look at a few of the major types of sacrifice in Old Testament times.

Types of sacrifice:
holocaust (burnt offering) Leviticus 1

In this sacrifice, an unblemished male animal, imaging Jesus the pure sacrifice, made atonement for the community's sins. The animal was burned entirely to show how our sin totally consumes the victim. There is one sacrifice, Christ, who was not consumed. He brought atonement to the world by conquering sin.

bread or cereal offering Leviticus 2

In this sacrifice, unleavened bread (2:4) is shaped into cakes or wafers and offered to the Lord. Unleavened bread is flat bread like the altar bread we use at Mass. A handful was burned on the altar and the rest was given to the priests (Aaron and his sons). It is a very holy oblation (meaning offering) because it images Christ in the Eucharist. Oil and frankincense (Leviticus 2:1) were placed on the bread prefiguring the worship and gifts that the Magi brought to the infant Jesus (Matthew 2:11). The bread was broken (Leviticus 2:6; 6:14) just as Jesus was broken on the cross and the Eucharist is broken into pieces during the Mass. This cereal offering was said to be a perpetual offering (Leviticus 6:11) and is continued today through the offering of the Mass.

communion (peace offering) Leviticus 3

Here the priest laid his hands on the animal, slaughtered (immolated) the animal, splashed the blood on the altar, and burned its fat on the altar. After this, the one who offered the sacrifice ate the rest of the sacrifice (less a portion for the priest) at a religious meal. The victim was shared between God and the one offering the victim. In this way they obtained communion with God. This sacrifice is similar to the others mentioned (all of which are related to Jesus' perfect sacrifice), but is unique in that it contains a communion meal. This meal should remind us of the Mass where Jesus the Victim is shared between God and the Church. Jesus offers Himself both to us, the Church, and to God the Father. We are united to God through this sacrifice and meal we call the Mass.

reparation (sin offering) Leviticus 4

When someone sinned, the prescribed kind of animal was brought to the meeting tent and slaughtered. Blood from the victim was sprinkled seven times toward the veil of the Holy of Holies behind which was the presence of God. Some of the blood was splashed on the altar and the fat was burned on the altar. Since sin shatters our relationship with God, the blood sprinkled toward his presence, the blood on the altar, and the fat offering to Him served as a sort of reunion with God. It atoned for sins, re-establishing the people's relationship with Him. The victim symbolizes Christ who was sacrificed for our sins (2 Corinthians 5:21; 1 John 2:2; Matthew 26:28) so that we could come back into communion with God.

thanks giving (todah)

See Leviticus 7:12-15; 22:29; 2 Chronicles 29:31; 33:16; Psalms. 50:14, 23; 56:12; 107:22; 116:17; Jeremiah 17:26; 33:11; and Amos 4:5

The Hebrew word "Todah" is usually translated "thank offering" or "thanks giving." As such it has a strong connection in name to our "Eucharist" which means "thanksgiving" in Greek. The Todah offering is a plea for God's deliverance and a thanks to the Lord for that forgiveness and deliverance that will come (see Psalms 22 and 69). Both the Todah and the Mass make use of Scripture and meal. Also, this Old Testament thanksgiving meal, united the participant with God and community much like our Mass does. The "thanks giving" or Todah sacrifice and our "thanksgiving" or Eucharistic sacrifice, both use bread and wine in the context of the communion meal. In the same way that our celebration of the Eucharist (the Mass) is the basis of our sacrificial life, the Todah was the basis of the Hebrew sacrificial life. Jewish rabbis prophesied that the Todah would go on until the end of time, and we see its continuance and fulfillment in our celebration of the Eucharist, the Mass.

All of these sacrifices, like our Mass today, required spotless victims (Leviticus 22:19) and pure participants (Leviticus 22:3). The Mass fulfills and transcends these Old Testament sacrifices because it brings into the present the perfect sacrificial self-offering of Jesus on the cross. There is no longer any need to sacrifice animals. Our New Covenant is sealed by the Blood of Jesus. In fact the Jews are no longer capable of sacrifice since the entire Jewish priesthood was wiped out by the Roman invasion of Jerusalem in 70 A.D.

Temple

The Roman invasion of 70 A.D. also destroyed the place where most sacrifices took place, the Jerusalem Temple. The Temple was originally built under King Solomon's rule and after being demolished, was rebuilt to its original beauty under King Herod. This huge structure, designed to remind the people of Heaven (Hebrews 9:23; Wisdom 9:8), was considered the center of religion, education, and politics.

The Temple consisted of a series of courtyards surrounding the Holy Place and the Holy of Holies. Inside of the Holy Place there was a gold (credence) table with bread and wine, a gold altar that never had a sacrifice on it, and a great seven branched candle stick (menorah). The showbread

(Leviticus 24:7) was offered to God as an everlasting agreement, now fulfilled by Jesus as the Bread of Life (John 6:35). The gold altar was empty because Jesus the Lamb of God had not yet been sacrificed. The Jewish rabbis before Christ believed the candles of the menorah foretold the Messiah (Hebrew for "anointed one") as the great light. We know that Christ (Greek for "anointed one") fulfilled this prophecy by being the "light of the world" (John 8:12).

Day of Atonement (Yom Kippur) Leviticus 16

In this once a year atonement for sin, the anointed and ordained priest put on particular holy vestments similar to those our priest wears and offered several different sacrifices to make atonement for sin. Just like the sacrifices described earlier, these sacrifices remind us of Christ who was sacrificed for our sins.

There are several things, though, that are unique to the Day of Atonement. First, this was the only time during the year when the priest went past the veil in the Holy of Holies to where the presence of the Lord was on the Ark of the Covenant. Next, the idea of the **scapegoat** comes from the Day of Atonement. The priest put both his hands on the goat's head and confessed the sins of the Israelites. This effectively put the sins of the people on the goat. Then it was sent out into the desert, taking all the people's sins away. Jesus, as you probably guessed from learning of the previous sacrifices, is the fulfillment of the scapegoat since He takes away our sins.

Suffering Servant Isaiah 42:1-9; 49:1-6; 50:4-11; 52:13 to 53:12

The songs of the suffering servant (those passages from Isaiah listed above) are some of the most well-known sections of the entire Old Testament. They foretell the coming of the Messiah as a servant of God who will bear the sins of the people. Jesus is this suffering servant, our Messiah who bore our sins so we could have eternal life. Let's check out how we can see this in the Gospels.

Suffering Servant in Isaiah	Jesus in the Gospels
delivering himself up to death (53:12)	delivered up to death
poured out (53:12)	poured out, that is, shed (Matthew 26:28)
Yet it was our infirmities that he bore, our sufferings that he endured (53:4) bearing sins of many (53:12)	He took away our infirmities and bore our diseases (Matthew 8:17) for forgiveness of sins (Matthew 26:28)
The suffering servant will be "a light for the nations" (42:6)	Jesus is "a light for revelation to the Gentiles" (Luke 2:32) The word for "Gentiles" and "nations" is the same in Greek.
He…was counted among the wicked (53:12)	He was counted among the wicked (Luke 22:37; 23:32)
Here is my servant whom I uphold, my chosen one with whom I am pleased, Upon whom I have put my spirit; he shall bring forth justice on the earth; the coastlands will wait for his teaching. (42:1-4)	Behold, my servant whom I have chosen, my beloved in whom I delight; I shall place my spirit upon him, and he will proclaim justice to the Gentiles…And in his name the Gentiles will hope. (Matthew 12:18-21) This is my beloved Son, with whom I am well pleased (Matthew 3:17 and 17:5)
Like a lamb led to slaughter or a sheep before the shearers, he was silent and opened not his mouth. (53:7)	And as he watched Jesus walk by, he said, 'Behold the Lamb of God.' (John 1:36). But he was silent and answered nothing. (Mk 14:61)

Prophecy of Malachi Chapter 1

Instead of offering the best animals from their flocks and herds, the Jews were sacrificing the animals that they didn't want. They offered the injured or sick animals, not the ones that image Christ as the pure and perfect sacrifice. This practice of offering imperfect animals was strictly forbidden (Deuteronomy 15:21 and Leviticus 3:1,6).

At this time, the Jews were God's chosen people and looked down upon the Gentiles (non-Jews). So when God said He would not accept his people's sacrifices but would find a pure offering from the Gentiles, the Jews must have gone nuts! They had lost their "most favored nation status" with God. They had kicked themselves out of the fold.

> God says, "from the rising of the sun, even to its setting, my name is great among the nations; And everywhere they bring sacrifice to my name, and a pure offering; For great is my name among the nations" (Malachi 1:11).

As noted earlier, "nations" and "Gentiles" is the same word in Greek and generally carries the same meaning. So in the passage from Malachi, God is saying that there will be a pure, universal offering among the Gentiles. It is universal in time and place, (from the rising of the sun to its setting, see Zechariah 8:7) and among people ("among the nations and everywhere"). This is strikingly opposed to what the Jews were accustomed to, since under the Law of Moses, sacrifice only took place in the Temple of Jerusalem (Deuteronomy 12:1-16) and the Gentiles were not allowed to participate (Leviticus 20:24; Deuteronomy 7:1; Ex 34:12). The prophecy of Malachi points to the age of the Messiah, Jesus, who will call people of all nations to the sacrifice of the Lord (see Micah 4:1-11; Zechariah 8:20; Isaiah 2:2). This sacrifice is his offering of Christ Himself on the cross and at Mass. The Didache, St. Irenaeus of Lyons, and Justin Martyr all point to the Mass as the fulfillment of the prophecy of

Malachi.[16] With Christ as our perfect offering, and over 300,000 Masses celebrated around the world each day, the Mass is clearly the pure and universal sacrifice prophesied in Malachi.

Synagogue

The word "synagogue" comes from Greek and means "gathering place" or "congregation." If at least ten Jewish men decided to gather together, they could form their own synagogue. This was a place where the Jewish people came together to pray and hear the scriptures. The synagogue was primarily a school. Sacrifice took place only in the Temple, not in synagogues. With the destruction of the Temple in 70 A.D., there was no place to sacrifice and the synagogues became the center of Jewish religious activity.

"In its characteristic structure the Liturgy of the Word originates in Jewish prayer."[17] As such, "A better knowledge of the Jewish people's faith and religious life as professed and lived even now can help our better understanding of certain aspects of Christian liturgy."[18] It may seem strange that looking at the Jewish faith can help us be better Christians, but keep an open mind and continue reading.

The early Christians "went to the temple area together every day, while in their homes they broke bread" (Acts 2:46). Did you notice that they still went to the Jewish Temple? Many Jewish beliefs and practices remained part of the early Christian's faith. We still read the Old Testament in our liturgies, use a cycle of readings to cover all the scriptures, and sing the holy, holy, holy—all of which were taken from Jewish liturgies. As time went on, however, Jewish authorities pushed Christians fully out of Judaism. Steven's martyrdom (Acts 7:59-60) and

---

16. Jurgens. *Faith of the Early Fathers* (Volume 1). Liturgical, pp. 4, 60, 95.
17. *Catechism of the Catholic Church*, par. 1096.
18. Ibid.

Saul's persecution (Acts 8:3) of Christians seen in the Acts of the Apostles were typical of the behavior that forced the split of Christianity from Judaism.

As mentioned earlier, the Christians did not leave empty handed. Along with the items named above, they took with them part of the synagogue service (which is focused on scripture) that was called the synaxis. This consisted of the same basic elements that our Liturgy of the Word contains: a greeting, readings and psalms, the sermon, prayers by and for the Church (prayers of the faithful), and the sign of peace. By tacking this scripture based service onto the Christian breaking of the bread (Eucharist), the early Christians had, by the end of the first century, shaped the basic structure of the Mass into the form we use today. So even in the very early times of the Church, the Mass was made up of the same two major parts that we see today: the Liturgy of the Word and Liturgy of the Eucharist.

Other Old Testament passages relevant to the Mass:
Genesis 31:54 Sacred Meal
Exodus 18:1-12 Jethro's sacrifices
Leviticus 23:13 Bread and wine offering
1 Sam 1:24 Sacrifice, bread (flour), and wine
1 Samuel 21 Possible holy bread multiplication
2 Sam 6 David prefigures Jesus as priest and king
1 Kings 19:4-8 Elijah and the bread from Heaven
2 Kings 4:42-44 Elisha's multiplication of loaves
Job 1:5; 42:7-9 Job's sacrifices
Psalm 116:12-13 Cup of salvation
Proverbs 9 The banquet of Wisdom
Isaiah 25:6-8 Heavenly Banquet
Isaiah 30:20 Bread (Eucharist) and water (Baptism)
Isaiah 55:1-3 Banquet of the Messiah

Jeremiah 33:11 Bridegroom (Christ), Bride (Church), and the people who todah (eucharistia) in the house of the Lord (church).

Hosea 9:4 Rejoice not, for no worship: no wine, no sacrifice, mourners' bread

Zechariah 9 Coming of the Messiah, drink blood like wine, altar, grain—bread, new wine—wine.

Responsorial Psalm (Gradual)

Psalm 110:1.2.3.4

Cantor: You are a priest forever, in the line of Melchizedek.

All: You are a priest forever, in the line of Melchizedek.

Cantor: The Lord said to my Lord: "Sit at my right hand till I make your enemies your footstool."

All: You are a priest forever, in the line of Melchizedek.

Cantor: The scepter of your power the Lord will stretch forth from Zion: "Rule in the midst of your enemies."

All: You are a priest forever, in the line of Melchizedek.

Cantor: "Yours is princely power in the day of your birth, in holy splendor; before the daystar, like the dew, I have begotten you."

All: You are a priest forever, in the line of Melchizedek.

Cantor: The Lord has sworn, and He will not repent. "You are a priest forever, according to the order of Melchizedek."

All: You are a priest forever, in the line of Melchizedek.

The Responsorial Psalm is, as the name suggests, generally taken from the Psalms of the Bible. It helps us to meditate on the First Reading while linking the Old and New Testaments. The ancient Jewish people used the Psalms in their worship services to break up the readings and allow participation. We do the same. In the Responsorial Psalm, we reflect upon what we heard in the reading and transform this reflection into a powerful prayer response. Our singing of the Psalm is this prayer. It may seem strange to think of singing as prayer, but Saint Augustine said that one who sings well prays twice.

Even better, the Psalms can be seen as love songs to God from his people. If two people are completely in love with each other and consequently want to bond themselves together forever, what do they do? They get married! Throughout all of salvation history, when God wants to show how completely He loves his people, He compares it to a marriage. That is why Scripture describes the union between God and his people as a marriage. In the Old Testament, God sought to make Israel his spouse (Hosea 2:21-22; Isaiah 54:5; 62:4-5; Jeremiah 2:2) and God the Son, Jesus, marries the New Israel, the Church, in the Mass (2 Corinthians 11:2; Ephesians 5:23-32; Rev 19:7-9; 21:2; 22:17). So just as the ancient Jews used the Psalms as love songs to their "husband" God, the **Responsorial Psalm can be seen as a love song** from the Bride, the Church, to her Groom, Christ.

Second Reading: 1 Corinthians 11:23-26

Reader: A reading from the first letter of Paul to the Corinthians.

I received from the Lord what I handed on to you, namely, that the Lord Jesus on the night in which he was betrayed took bread, and after he had given thanks, broke it and said, "This is my Body, which is for you. Do this in remembrance of me." In the same way, after the supper, He took the cup, saying, "This cup is the new covenant in my Blood. Do this, whenever you drink it, in remembrance of me." Every time, then, you eat this bread and drink this cup, you proclaim the death of the Lord until He comes!

Reader: The word of the Lord.

All: Thanks be to God.

Listen to the reader. Is the Word of God being proclaimed or merely read like a math textbook? Does the reader understand what he or she is saying? Is he or she putting people to sleep?

Is the scripture touching the peoples' hearts? How might you improve on the proclamation of the Scripture passage if you were the reader? What do you think it was like to listen to Jesus read scripture (Luke 4:16-22)? What words should be emphasized? What is the passage trying to tell us?

The **second reading is taken from part of the New Testament outside of the Gospels**, usually from one of St. Paul's letters or the catholic letters.

New Testament Background of the Mass

"Do this…in remembrance of Me. For as often as you eat this bread and drink this cup, you proclaim the death of the Lord until He comes" (1 Corinthians 11:25-26). We all know the context. Christ uttered these words at the Last Supper and how did the early Christians respond? "They devoted themselves to the apostles' teaching and fellowship, to the breaking of bread and the prayers…Day by day, attending the temple together and breaking bread in their homes, they partook of food with glad and generous hearts" (Acts 2:42, 46). The early Christians' most important gathering came on "the first day of the week," Sunday, where they met "to break bread" (Acts 20:7). So from the earliest times of Christianity until the present, the Eucharistic celebration, which is called the Mass for those of us in the Latin rite, has remained the center of the Church's life.[19]

Acts of the Apostles 2:42-47; 20:7-11

The Acts of the Apostles gives us a glimpse into the life of the early Church. We can begin to understand the Apostles' theology as we see how they handled certain issues that arose. For instance, we see that those who accepted the Apostles' message were baptized and "devoted themselves to the teachings of the Apostles and to the communal life, to the breaking of the bread and to the prayers" (Acts 2:42).

---

19. Adapted from the *Catechism of the Catholic Church*, par. 1342-1343.

To understand this passage better, look at its parts. They, the newly baptized Christians, "devoted themselves." They weren't just interested in it or liked it, they "devoted themselves." So what did they devote themselves to? "[T]he teachings of the Apostles and…the breaking of the bread." These are the two items that we need to understand fully.

What did the teachings of the Apostles become? They can now be found in the New Testament of the Bible. So the early Christians were getting their daily dose of God's word through the teachings of the Apostles.

What was that other item? It was the breaking of the bread. The early Christians used this term instead of Eucharistic Celebration. So when these are put together we see Christians coming together (communal life) for prayer, God's word, and the Eucharistic celebration. This combination of word and sacrament should always remind us of the Mass with its two key parts: the Liturgy of the Word and the Liturgy of the Eucharist.

Moving just a few verses down, we see that "Every day" these same new Christians "devoted themselves to meeting together in the temple area and to breaking bread in their homes" (Acts 2:46). It's clear that at this point they were still tied to Judaism (the Jewish faith), for they prayed every day in Herod's Temple in Jerusalem. As noted earlier, the Christians worshipped with the Jewish people for years before separating. And what was the other thing that they did daily? It was the breaking of the bread, the Eucharist, the Mass.

The next passage we will look at from the Acts of the Apostles is for all of you who teach, give homilies or talks, or anything similar. One Sunday (On the first day of the week Acts 20:7) at Mass (break bread Acts 20:7) while St. Paul was preaching, a boy who was sitting on a window sill fell asleep and tumbled out of the third story window. Can you imagine how embarrassed St. Paul must have been! St. Paul was able to restore him to life, but I always feel better about my own teaching when I hear that some people fell asleep even during St. Paul's sermons! Maybe I'm not such a boring teacher after all!

First Letter to the Corinthians Chapters 10 & 11

This letter by St. Paul contains valuable Eucharistic texts that cover the institution of the Eucharist at the Last Supper, the mystical body of Christ (the Church), and unworthy participation in the Eucharist.

In the midst of warning the Corinthians not to participate in idolatry, St. Paul utters these rich words, "The cup of blessing that we bless, is it not a participation in the blood of Christ? The bread that we break, is it not a participation in the body of Christ?" In this one phrase he simultaneously speaks of both the sacramental Body of Christ, the Eucharist, and the mystical body of Christ (see 1 Corinthians 12:12-27), the Church.

In the next chapter, chapter eleven, St. Paul objects to the Corinthians' unholy celebration of the Mass. Reminding them that, "the Lord Jesus, on the night he was handed over, took bread, and, after he had given thanks, broke it and said, 'This is my body that is for you. Do this in remembrance of me.' In the same way also the cup, after supper, saying, 'This cup is the new covenant in my blood. Do this, as often as you drink it, in remembrance of me.' For as often as you eat this bread and drink the cup, you proclaim the death of the Lord until he comes" (1 Corinthians 11:23-26). St. Paul hoped this would bring them back to consideration for their fellow neighbor and to reverence for the Eucharist. But just in case that didn't work, he showed them that "whoever eats the bread or drinks the cup of the Lord unworthily will have to answer for the body and blood of the Lord. A person should examine himself, and so eat the bread and drink the cup. For anyone who eats and drinks without discerning the body, eats and drinks judgment on himself" (1 Corinthians 11:27-29).

When speaking of the body of Christ, this passage, like the earlier passage, points both to the Eucharist and the Church. It clarifies the intimate connection between the two. This reminds us that before receiving Communion, we need to realize that Jesus is present in the Eucharist and be in union with the Church.

Book of Hebrews

What does the Book of Hebrews have to offer us? It provides us with another look at Melchizedek typology and at the relation between Old Testament animal sacrifices and the sacrifice of Christ.

The image of Jesus as high priest is found early (2:17; 3:1) and often in the Book of Hebrews. The fact that Jesus is high priest should tell us something, namely, He offers sacrifice. As mentioned previously, sacrifice is what distinguishes a priest from a non-priest. It is the root of all priesthood. As the Book of Hebrews puts it, "[E]very high priest is appointed to offer gifts and sacrifices; thus the necessity for this one also to have something to offer" (Hebrews 8:3). What is it then that this one, Jesus our high priest, offers as sacrifice? Well, let me sidestep that question right now and come back to it in a minute.

We first need to understand "When there is a change in priesthood, there is necessarily a change of law as well" (Hebrews 7:12). Jesus wasn't part of the priesthood of his day, the levitical (7:11) priesthood. Instead He reintroduced the old priesthood of Melchizedek (5:5-6 and later 6:20). The priesthood of Melchizedek actually predated the levitical priesthood but had been lost since Melchizedek's time. The author of Hebrews provides in chapter seven an excellent comparison between Melchizedek and Jesus much like the one we looked at in the Meal of Melchizedek section. Along came Jesus whose reviving of the priesthood according to Melchizedek necessitated a change of covenant law. It is appropriate that Jesus is also "mediator of a better covenant, enacted on better promises" (Hebrews 8:6). The law of this new and better covenant is put on the people's minds and written on their hearts (Hebrews 8:10).

Now let's go back to our question. Knowing that not even the old covenant was sealed without the shedding of blood (Hebrews 9:18), where is our bloody sacrifice for this new covenant? What sacrifice does Christ, our high priest, have to offer? Well, Jesus sealed it "not with the blood of goats and calves but with his own blood, thus obtaining eternal redemption" (Hebrews 9:12). Thus Jesus is High Priest, mediator of the New Covenant, and Victim or Sacrifice of that covenant all at the same time. He was sacrificed on the altar of the cross and that sacrifice is made present to us today in the Mass. Jesus is also the priest for his own sacrifice at the Mass, for as St. Thomas Aquinas says,

> "Christ is the source of all priesthood: the priest of the old law was a figure of Christ, and the priest of the new law acts in the person of Christ."[20]

Saint Cyprian of Carthage adds:

> "For, if Christ Jesus, our Lord and God, is himself the High Priest of God the Father, and first offered himself as a sacrifice to his Father and commanded this to be done in commemoration of himself, certainly the priest who imitates that which Christ did and then offers the true and full sacrifice in the Church of God the Father, if he thus begins to offer according to what he sees Christ himself offered, performs truly in the place of Christ."[21]

So although we see our earthly priests celebrating Mass, they are acting in persona Christi. Jesus our Heavenly priest is the true priest acting through the earthly substitutes.

One may ask, "If the sacrifice of the cross is all sufficient why is there a need for a commemorative sacrifice of the Mass?" In the sacrifice of the Mass graces of the cross from which the Mass gets its power are applied to you! "For it is the liturgy through which, especially in the divine sacrifice of the Eucharist, 'the work of our redemption is accomplished.'"[22] The objection may continue, "Yeah, but aren't you Catholics re-crucifying Christ every time you say Mass? Don't you know He was sacrificed once

---

20. *Catechism of the Catholic Church*, par. 1548 (STh III, 22, 4c.).
21. Jurgens. *Faith of the Early Fathers* (Volume 1). Liturgical, p. 233.
22. *Constitution on the Sacred Liturgy*, art. 2.

and for all (Hebrews 7:27)?" We are not re-crucifying Christ (Hebrews 6:6) in the Mass, He is sacrificed once and for all, but you must understand what this means.

This phrase "once and for all" does not mean once and it's over, it means once and continuing for all time. Take a look at chapter nine of the Book of Hebrews where the author of Hebrews writes that Christ "entered once and for all into the sanctuary" (Hebrews 9:12). "For Christ did not enter into a sanctuary made by hands, a copy of the true one, but heaven itself, that he may now appear before God on our behalf" (Hebrews 9:24). If Christ is still in the sanctuary of Heaven appearing before God on our behalf years after He offered Himself on the cross, then his sacrifice didn't take place once and then end. It takes place once and never ends.

Therefore "once and for all" means his offering is eternal. Jesus hasn't left Heaven. He is still there offering Himself for us, although not in a painful manner as He did on the cross. This is why we can receive the grace of the cross now although Jesus lived long ago. If Jesus' death and Resurrection were only historical, what effect could they have now? None at all. But the historical crucifixion is coupled with Christ's eternal self-offering which transcends time. Therefore no matter what time period a person lives in, Christ's saving grace can become present to that person. Stated another way, Jesus' sacrificial self-offering is still going on. You can't repeat something that never ends.

> "His Paschal mystery is a real event that occurred in our history, but it is unique: all other historical events happen once, and then they pass away, swallowed up in the past. The Paschal mystery of Christ, by contrast, cannot remain only in the past, because by his death he destroyed death, and all that Christ is—all that he did and suffered for all men—participates in the divine eternity, and so transcends all times while being made present in them all."[23]

---

23. *Catechism of the Catholic Church*, par. 1085.

So the sacrifice of Christ didn't stop on the cross (Rev 5:6). The perpetuity of this sacrifice was demonstrated in the Mass of the early Church by placing a small amount of consecrated bread from one day's Mass in the chalice on the next day. This showed that all Masses are united and the sacrifice of Christ is never ending.

The Eucharist is present in eternity and is present in history in three ways. It's prefigured in the Old Testament, fulfilled as an event in the New, and in our time made present as a sacrament. The Eucharist is this sacrament that makes the sacrifice present to us.

Your "homework" for this section is to find out what the author of Hebrews means when he writes, "We should not stay away from our assembly" (Hebrews 10:25).

Book of Revelation

Also see CCC 1137-1139

If Mass is the one thing all Catholics are familiar with, then the Book of Revelation has to be the one thing all Catholics know nothing about. This little venture into the Book of Revelation, which is also called the Apocalypse, is by no means a complete look at the book, but it may begin to unlock a few of the book's mysteries. The aim in our look at Revelation is to come to an understanding that, "In the earthly liturgy we take part in a foretaste of [the] heavenly liturgy."[24] Pope John Paul II has called the Mass "Heaven on earth,"[25] and this is not a new concept, it was also a belief held by many early Church fathers. But most Catholics would say when they picture Heaven, they have something better in mind than Mass. So why should anyone believe such a crazy proposition? The rest of this section is one long answer to that question.

---

24. *Constitution on the Sacred Liturgy*, art. 8.
25. Hahn. *Lamb's Supper*. Doubleday, p. 3. (Angelus Address, Nov. 3, 1996).

The main activities of the book of Revelation take place in Heaven (Rev 4:1-2), an environment full of liturgy. Liturgical celebration, you will remember, is community worship of God based on some pattern or ritual. The Mass is the liturgy that we as Catholics most frequently take part in. So take a look at this list of liturgical items and actions from the book of Revelation and compare them to your experience of liturgy.[26]

Revelation chp. & vs.	Subject of the section
1:10	**Sunday worship** The early Christians used term "Lord's Day" to refer to the first day of the week, Sunday.
1:13	**High Priest** Jesus, the Son of Man (Mk 8:31), is dressed in the garments of the high priest of the Temple. He is our high priest (Hebrews 4:14).
1:6; 4:4; 4:10; 5:8; 5:10; 7:11; 11:16; 19:4; 20:6	**Priests** The Greek word "presbyteroi" is often translated "elders" yet we derive the English word "priest" from this same Greek word. Thus at times it may be better to translate the word as "priest" rather than "elder."
1:13; 3:4; 3:18; 4:4; 6:11; 7:9; 15:6; 19:13-14 22:14	**Liturgical Vestments** Special garments have always been part of liturgy. White robes (albs), sashes (stoles?), etceteras are still used today. 14:3-4 **Celibacy** The 144,000 are symbolically called virgins. They had not worshipped false gods.
6:9; 8:3-4; 11:1; 14:18; 16:7	**Altar** Always indicating sacrifice, the altar points to Christ's sacrifice (Rev 5:6) and the martyrs who joined their sufferings to those of the Lamb.

---

26. The following section relies heavily on the work of Dr. Scott Hahn in *The Lamb's Supper, pp. 119-120.* All of Dr. Hahn's works on the Mass are outstanding.

4:6; 21:6; 22:1	*Sea of Glass* like crystal and the river of life giving water point to the purification waters of the Jerusalem Temple, the waters of Baptism, and the baptismal pools that we now use.
1:12; 2:5; 4:5	*Lamp Stands* These would remind the early Christian reader of the seven branched Menorah which had at one time been in the Temple but had been missing for over 500 years when Revelation was written. The flaming torches and Menorah should not only remind us of the candles we use in Mass but also should remind us of Jesus, the light of the world (John 8:12).
5:8; 8:3-5	*Incense* The incense we use in Mass symbolizes the prayers of the saints which rise up to God (see Psalm 141:2).
15:2-3	*Music* Revelation speaks of worshipping God with harps and singing. Harps were the common liturgical music instruments of the day. Our Mass today is full of music.
1:4	*Greeting* The Mass often begins with the same greeting (with slight modifications) that John starts his letter with. In the Mass, the priest says, "grace and peace of God our Father and the Lord Jesus Christ be with you." John begins his letter with the greeting, "grace to you and peace from him who is and who was and who is to come…and from Jesus Christ."
Chapters 2 and 3	*Penitence* In the letters to the seven churches, the word "repent" is used repeatedly. This should remind us of the Penitential Rite of the Mass where we repent and are forgiven of our (venial) sins.

15:3-4	**_The Gloria_** Angels play harps and sing words we hear in the Gloria, "for you alone are holy." Both our Gloria and the angels in Revelation praise God, worshipping the Father and the Lamb in song.
19:1,3,4,6	**_The Alleluia_** In Revelation and in the Mass, the Alleluia is used to introduce the good news, that is, the Gospel.
1:11; 5:1; 10:2,9; 20:12	**_Scrolls_** were the "books" in the days before there were bound books as we have them now. Because there were no printing presses in those times, the scrolls had to be hand copied. This made scrolls rare and very expensive. Few people owned scrolls for personal reading. The mention of a scroll would have undoubtedly made people think of the synagogues, the Temple, or their new local church (which may have been in someone's house) where the scriptures of the Old Testament were read to them from papyrus scrolls. So the people would have had liturgy on their minds at the mention of scrolls.
Rev. 1:1,3	**_Revelation_** The book of Revelation takes its name from the announcement (1:1) that it is the "revelation of Jesus Christ." In verse three, we find a blessing on the person who reads the letter out loud and on the people to listen to the reader. Surely then, the letter was intended to be read and heard by the Christian people in their liturgical assembly, the Mass.

1:10; 11:12; 21:9-10	***Going to Heaven*** Several times in the book of Revelation we see people going up into Heaven. At the beginning of the Eucharistic Prayer in the Mass, we lift our hearts up to the Lord, joining in the heavenly worship.
4:8	***The Holy, Holy, Holy*** (Sanctus) Later in the Mass we join in this prayer that the angels and saints sing constantly in Heaven.
2:17	***The Hidden Manna*** After speaking about food sacrificed to idols, the topic turns to true sacrifice to God, the Hidden Manna. Hidden Manna probably at one time referred to Passover bread and later, in John's time, was a name for the Eucharist.
15:7; ch. 16; 21:9	***Gold Bowls*** These were a sort of shallow chalice. They are associated with the gold chalices that our priests use in Mass.
12:1-17; 5:8; 6:9-19: 8:3-4; 12:7; 21:14	***Saints*** We, in the Mass, invoke the prayers of many of the holy people that are mentioned in Revelation: the Virgin Mary, St. Michael the archangel, the Apostles and the martyrs.
7:12; 19:4; 22:21	***The Great Amen*** We imitate those saints in Heaven by using the "Amen" to give assent to prayers.
5:6 and 27 other times	***The Lamb of God*** In Mass we also recall that Jesus is the Lamb who takes away the sins of the world.
Chapters 19 and 21	***Wedding Supper of the Lamb*** When we consume Holy Communion we consummate the union with Christ. In other words, our eating of the Flesh and Blood of Jesus seals the wedding between Christ and the Church.

After looking at the above, I'm sure you'll concur that the scene in the Book of Revelation is certainly liturgical. Not only that but you probably noticed that this liturgy in Heaven is remarkably similar to the Mass. This is not mere coincidence. Mass is Heaven on earth.

The structure of the Book of Revelation also is similar to that of the Mass. The Book opens with a greeting from St. John that is also used (with slight adjustment) as an opening greeting in Mass, wishing grace and peace on the people from God our Father and the Lord Jesus Christ (Rev 1:4). Revelation is then concerned with the repentance of the seven churches, while the Mass proceeds into the Penitential Rite which calls for the repentance of the congregation. The rest of the Apocalypse, like the Mass, can by easily divided in half. The first eleven chapters pertain to the proclamation of the letters to the seven churches and the opening of the scroll. This emphasis on readings makes this first part a close match to the Liturgy of the Word, the first of the two main parts of the Mass. The second half of the Book of Revelation begins in chapter 11 and finds its fulfillment in the pouring of the chalices and the Marriage Supper of the Lamb. With these qualities, the second half shows a striking resemblance to the second part of the Mass, the Liturgy of the Eucharist.

Clearly there is a strong connection between the liturgy of Heaven and our Mass. In fact, "by the Eucharistic celebration we already unite ourselves with the heavenly liturgy and anticipate eternal life, when God will be all in all."[27]

As mentioned previously, the liturgy in Heaven is the wedding supper of the Lamb (Revelation 19:7,9; 21:2,9,17) and our union with Jesus in the Eucharist is the seal of that marriage. This marital union is not some crazy new concept that I dreamed up. In the Old Testament, we often find God "marrying" his people, the Israelites, (essentially the Old Testament Church) (Hosea 2:16-22; Is 54:5-6; 62:5; Ezekiel 16:6-14). Our Catholic Church is the full flowering of the Old Testament Bride (2 Corinthians

---

27. *Catechism of the Catholic Church*, par. 1326.

11:2; Ephesians 5:22-27; Gal 4:26). "The Church is his beloved Bride who calls to her Lord and through him offers worship to the eternal Father."[28] She has been joined to her Savior in the closest way possible, a marriage covenant.

The following comparison may help:

Earthly (natural) Wedding	*Heavenly (supernatural) Wedding*
Groom has tremendous desire to love	Christ has a tremendous desire to love
Bride needs the love of her groom	Church needs the love of Christ
There is a tradition associated with weddings in which the groom carries bride across the threshold of the honeymoon suite.	In the heavenly wedding, the Groom, Christ, carries his Bride, the Church, across the threshold. What does this mean? The altar is the threshold between earth and Heaven. So Jesus carries us, his Bride, to Heaven through the actions on the altar at Mass. That's a powerful statement! But we already knew that. For we know that by eating his Flesh and drinking his Blood which come to us on the altar, we receive the grace for eternal life (John 6:54).
is sealed with a covenant in liturgy (Mass)	is sealed with a covenant in liturgy (Mass)
requires a total self-offering from both the bride and the groom	requires a total self-offering from both the Bride (Church) and the Groom (Jesus)

---

28. *Constitution on the Sacred Liturgy*, art. 7 and *Catechism of the Catholic Church*, par. 1089.

| at the consummation, when the groom totally gives himself to the bride, he says to her, "This is my body," and then she receives him with love | at the consummation, when the Groom totally gives Himself to the Bride, He says to her, "This is my Body," and then she receives Him with love |
| God has a need for people so He says to all brides and grooms, "go forth and multiply" | God has a need for people (covenant Family) so Christ says to the Church, "go make disciples of all nations" |

This event, the wedding feast, shows itself to be the pinnacle of the Book of Revelation.

Other New Testament passages relevant to the Mass:
Acts 27:35 St. Paul celebrates the Eucharist
1 Colossians 1:12-20 possible early Eucharistic Prayer
Jude v12 Agape feasts

Alleluia

Cantor: Alleluia (Revelation 19:1).
All: Alleluia.
Cantor: I am the living bread from heaven, says the Lord; if anyone eats this bread he will live for ever (John 6:51).
All: Alleluia.

The word "Alleluia" is an old Jewish expression meaning "Praise God!" It should be sung in every season outside of Lent.

Priest/Deacon: The Lord be with you.
All: And also with you.
Priest/Deacon: A reading from the holy gospel according to Luke.
All: Glory to you, Lord.

While saying "Glory to you, Lord" a small cross is traced on the fore-head, on the lips, and over the heart. The first cross we trace asks the Lord to be on our minds or in our thoughts. The second requests that He be in everything we say, letting the lips proclaim what the mind contains. The third cross invites Him into our hearts.

Gospel Luke 9:11-17

Priest/Deacon: Jesus spoke to the crowds of the reign of God, and healed all who were in need of healing. As sunset approached the Twelve came and said to Him, "Dismiss the crowd so that they can go into the villages and farms in the neighborhood and find themselves lodging and food, for this is certainly an out-of-the-way place." He answered them, "Why do you not give them some-thing to eat yourselves?" They replied, "We have nothing but five loaves and two fishes. Or shall we ourselves go and buy food for all these people?" (There were about five thousand men.) Jesus said to his disciples, "Have them sit down in groups of fifty or so." They followed his instructions and got them all seated. Then, taking the five loaves and the two fishes, Jesus raised his eyes to heaven, pronounced a blessing over them, broke them, and gave them to his disciples for distribution to the crowd. They all ate until they had enough. What they had left, over and above, filled twelve baskets.

The gospel of the Lord.

(Priest kisses the book) After reading Gospel, the priest "kisses the book, saying inaudibly: Through the words of the gospel may our sins be washed away."[29]

All: Praise to you, Lord Jesus Christ.

Through the word of God we come to know the Word who is God. This means that in hearing and understanding the Scriptures (word of God) that are read to us, we come to know about and have a relationship

---

29. *General Instruction of the Roman Missal (2000)*, no. 134.

with the Son of God (the Eternal Word, who is the second Person of the Trinity and assumed a human nature as Jesus). For "Jesus…is, in fact, the Word of God made man for the salvation of all."[30] So as the priest kisses the book of Scripture from which he read, we know that he does this because his heart overflows with love for Jesus (the Eternal Word) who the priest learned about through the Scriptures (word of God). The word of God, Sacred Scripture, is meant for all of us. If we had time it would be appropriate for every person in the congregation to kiss the book of Gospels at Mass. Since time does not permit this, the priest stands in our place kissing the Gospel book.

The high point in the Scriptures, the Gospels, show us the Eternal Word (John 1:14) of God, Jesus Christ. The word of God, Sacred Scripture, stands in the place of the Eternal Word of God, Jesus. So when the priest kisses the Gospel book, we see a representative (the priest) of the Church, the bride of the Lamb, kissing her Groom Christ as represented by the Gospel book. Notice the similarity and yet reversal from the priest kissing the altar at the beginning of Mass where the priest symbolized Christ and the altar symbolized the heart of the Church.

But the altar is symbolic of many things besides the heart of the Church. For instance, in the Sinai Covenant sacrifice (Exodus 24) we saw that the altar stands for God the Father. On the right hand of the Father (left for those of us in the congregation facing the altar) is where the lectern is most commonly placed. This of course is where we learned about Jesus the Eternal Word through the readings of the word of God (Bible) in the Liturgy of the Word. Thus Jesus, represented by the lectern where the word is read, is at the right hand of the Father, represented by the altar.

Always remember that **the word of God is meant to live in the heart, not merely on the printed page**. The Bible is a tool to put the word of God on your heart. And as St. Jerome puts it, "Ignorance of scripture is

---

30. *Dominus Iesus*, 10.

ignorance of Christ." So listen closely and pray that you may understand and live the message that this "good news" or Gospel presents. Because the Gospel is the high point of the Liturgy of the Word, great reverence should be shown during the proclamation of the Gospel passage. In the Middle Ages, princes would remove their crowns, knights would draw their swords from their sheaths (yes, just like the Knights of Columbus) and remove their gloves, and regular men would remove their headgear. We stand during the Gospel and the Creed because standing is the position of reverent attention. Why do we not kneel? Because the Gospel calls us to action and standing shows that we are ready to quickly respond to this call.

Gospel Background of the Mass

The Gospels are the full flowering of God's revelation to us. They present us with the most complete picture we have of who Jesus really is. If we search Sacred Scripture with dedication, it will show us that He can be found in the Mass. We will come to know Him in the breaking of the bread (Luke 24:35).

Wedding Feast

Read Matthew 9:14-15, Mark 2:18-20 and Luke 5:34; Matthew 19:6; Matthew 22:1-14; Matthew 25:1-13; Luke 5:34; Luke 13:15-19; Luke 14:8-24; John 2:3-10; John 3:28-30

In our last look into scripture passages related to the Mass, the wedding supper in the book of Revelation was presented. In the Gospels, this wedding supper theme can be seen in several different passages. The key to understanding them is the same key that was used in the Book of Revelation, namely, this wedding feast is related to Heaven. The passages stress the idea that we must be ready (unlike the people in Matthew 25:1-13) and willing (unlike the people in Matthew 22:3) to accept the invitation to the wedding feast in the kingdom of Heaven. They also remind us that the Mass is the wedding supper of the Lamb.

The most significant of the Gospel texts on wedding feasts is not a parable but an actual event, the wedding feast at Cana. Found in chapter two of John's Gospel, this passage tells of Jesus' first public miracle, changing water into wine. This miracle prefigures Christ's changing of wine into his Blood at the Last Supper and the same transformation at our Mass. It is also related to Moses' first miracle, changing of water into blood (Exodus 7:20). In the miracle at Cana, Jesus gives the people about 135 gallons of wine to drink. This abundance in drink should remind us of the abundance of food Jesus provided when He multiplied the loaves.

Multiplication of the Loaves

Matthew 14:15-21; Matthew 15:32-39; Mark 6:32-44,52; Mark 8:1-10; Luke 9:10-17, John 6:1-15;

Have you ever noticed that Jesus is always talking about food in the Gospels? It seems like every time you turn around He and his Apostles are eating again. I'm not implying anything about their weight, I am simply wondering why He speaks of food so much (and who got all of the leftovers from the multiplication of the loaves and fish).

We don't have space to analyze every reference to food in the New Testament, but let's look at the feeding miracles to see what insight they may bring us about the most holy Mass.

Without a doubt, these miracles are strongly linked to the Old Testament. For instance, 2 Kings 4:42-44 tells of Elisha multiplying loaves. These loaves were made of barley, his servant doubted that the few loaves would satisfy all the people, and after it was done, there were leftovers. In John 6:1-15 Jesus multiplies barley loaves, Philip doubts that the few loaves would be enough but after everyone eats, there is plenty of leftovers.

The miracles of multiplication in the New Testament are also linked with the manna in the desert found in the Old Testament. In the Old

Testament, God gave his people who were in the desert manna and quail. Jesus gave his people who followed Him into the desert bread and fish. The field in which Jesus multiplied loaves was not arid but grassy showing his fruitfulness and life. In the desert, there was never any leftover manna, but in greener pastures, Christ's abundance overflows into many baskets of leftovers. Thus the multiplication miracles in the New Testament are meant to show us Jesus is more powerful than the Old Testament miracle workers.

Bread and fish have since the early times of Christianity been symbols for Christ Himself (John 6:48 and Ichthys). Jesus multiplied loaves and fish on at least two different occasions. The first one can be found in Mark 6, Matthew 14, Luke 9, and John 6. This instance is the feeding of 5,000 men plus women and children with only five loaves and two fish. The numbers in the passage are very significant. The number five may have some connection to five Jewish patriarchs who fathered the Jewish people or five covenants that God made with the Israelites. The 12 baskets of fragments that are collected point to the 12 tribes of Israel. Further, Jesus has the crowd sit in groups reminiscent of the way the Israelites camped in groups in the desert. Thus in the first miracles there is a strong Jewish connection. Jesus is feeding the Jewish people.

In the second miracle, found in Mark 8 and Matthew 15, Jesus feeds 4,000 men plus women and children with only seven loaves of bread and a few fish. The number four is connected to the four corners of the earth, meaning everything on the earth. The number seven symbolizes completeness, universality, or perfection, so the seven loaves and the seven baskets of fragments relate to the extension of the kingdom to all people. Christ now feeds everyone.

All of the feeding miracles also display a strong connection to the first Mass, the Last Supper. Jesus uses the same fourfold pattern in the feeding miracles and in the Last Supper (see Matthew 26:26 for example). This formula or pattern is:

Take, Bless, Break, Give

In our Mass, these become present the following actions:

  Take–procession with gifts, preparation of the altar and the placement of gifts on the altar

  Bless—Eucharistic Prayer

  Break—Fraction rite (Lamb of God)

  Give/Share—communion

Like those few loaves and fish given to such large crowds, our goodness in and of itself could never possibly accomplish much. But Jesus helps us by "multiplying" our goodness so that we can spiritually feed even the largest of crowds.

Bread of Life Discourse John 6

As mentioned earlier, one of these feeding miracles is found in the sixth chapter of John's Gospel. That account of a multiplication miracle ends just a few verses from where our next topic, the Bread of Life discourse, picks up.

I can't stress enough how important it is for you to read the sixth chapter of John's Gospel. Every Catholic should know it well. Christ's presence in the Eucharist is explained so well there in John's Gospel that I feel like anything I say about the passage will be pale and superfluous. Consequently, I'll try to limit my own comments in this section to a brief overview of the passage and with the rest of the space allow the early Church Fathers to give more meaningful commentary.

The heart of the passage begins in verse twenty-six, where we see the Jews have followed Jesus because He gave them bread at the multiplication miracle mentioned earlier in the chapter. Jesus points out they are in the wrong frame of mind, thinking of their physical needs rather than their spiritual necessities. He leads them in the right direction (6:27,29), showing the Jews that He will fill their souls with grace so they can reach eternal life in Heaven. In verse 30 the Jews have realized that Jesus is asserting that He is the Messiah and they ask Him to prove it. The Jews expected the

Messiah to bring back the manna that God fed them with in the desert (Ex 16:1-16,35). So in essence they asked, "If you are the Messiah, then prove it by giving us the bread from heaven, the manna." Jesus tells them of a greater bread, the True Bread from Heaven. So the Jews ask for it. Then Jesus throws them off balance with the words, "I am the bread of life" (vs. 35). The Jews question Him, but Jesus reinforces his statement, "I am the bread of life" (48). He links this True Bread to the manna but also makes it clear that this new Bread supersedes the old because He is this True Bread from Heaven.

He goes on to assert if you eat the Bread you will have eternal life. Again the Jews question his sayings, asking how He could give them his Flesh. In response, Jesus uses several different ways to make the same basic message clear: 1) He is the True Bread from Heaven, 2) this Bread is his Flesh, 3) you must eat his Flesh and drink his Blood to go to Heaven. The Jews were shocked. While they saw blood as a source of life, this eating of flesh and drinking blood stood directly opposed to their beliefs (Leviticus 17:14). Many of his disciples left (6:66) and Jesus even asked his Apostles if they wanted to leave (6:67)! This was obviously very important to Jesus.

So what do the early Church Fathers have to say about the Eucharist? St. Ignatius of Antioch, one who learned from the mouth of St. John himself, calls the Eucharist the "medicine of immortality, the antidote against death, enabling us to live forever in Jesus Christ."[31] Roughly a hundred years later, Tertullian comments that "the flesh feeds on the Body and Blood of Christ that the soul too may be fattened on God."[32] St. Cyprian of Carthage states:

> "As the prayer continues, we ask and say, 'Give us this day our daily bread.'…And we ask that this bread be given us daily, so that we who are in Christ and daily receive the Eucharist as the food of

---

31. Jurgens. *Faith of the Early Fathers* (Volume 1). Liturgical, p. 19.
32. Ibid. P. 149.

salvation, may not, by falling into some more grievous sin and then in abstaining from communicating, be withheld from the heavenly Bread, and be separated from Christ's Body.... He Himself warns us, saying, 'Unless you eat the flesh of the Son of Man and drink His blood, you shall not have life in you.' Therefore do we ask that our Bread, which is Christ, be given to us daily, so that we who abide and live in Christ may not withdraw from His sanctification and from His Body."[33]

And finally St. Cyril of Jerusalem, speaking of the Eucharist, says,

"Tell me: if someone gave you some grains of gold, would you not hold them with all carefulness, lest you might lose something of them and thereby suffer a loss? Will you not, therefore, be much more careful in keeping watch over what is more precious than gold and gems, so that not a particle of it may escape you?"[34]

This powerful belief in Jesus' Real Presence in the Eucharist will make Mass a vibrant force in anyone's life. The Eucharist is the central Mystery of Faith and the greatest treasure of the Church,[35] yet we know that many Catholics today have a lack of Eucharistic 'hunger' and 'thirst.' They see going to Communion as no big deal. But now it's our turn to evangelize, to instill in others the desire for Christ's Body and Blood. Will you accept the challenge of Christ's Gospel?

Last Supper Matthew 26, Mark 14, Luke 22

As mentioned earlier, the first Mass and the beginnings of our priest-hood can be traced back to the Last Supper. The Mass is the renewal of the covenant sealed at the Last Supper just as the Seder (Passover) meal

---

33. Jurgens. *Faith of the Early Fathers* (Volume 1). Liturgical, p. 223.
34. Jurgens. Faith of the Early Fathers (Volume 1). Liturgical, p. 366.
35. Adapted from Paul VI. *Mystery of Faith*. St. Paul, p. 5.

renewed the covenant sealed at the original Passover. We are all familiar with what took place on that Holy Thursday in the upper room: Jesus met with his 12 Apostles to commemorate the Passover and in doing so He also gave us the Eucharist. For Jews, the Passover meant freedom from slavery to the Egyptians. For Christians, the new Passover, the Eucharistic Celebration, means freedom from slavery to sin and death. Let's take a closer look at the Last Supper's relation to the Passover and the Mass.

Luke 22:7-15, Mark 14:12-16, and Matthew 26:17-19 all make it clear that the Last Supper takes place in a Passover meal (also called Seder). Other than the preparation for the meal, found in Mark 14:13-15 and Luke 22:10-12, the beginning part of the meal is not described in detail in the synoptic Gospels. In Matthew 26:21, it is clear that they have already started their Seder meal.

Verse 26 in chapter 26 of Matthew's Gospel brings the first important element forth as it relates, "While they were eating, Jesus took bread, said the blessing, broke it, and giving it to his disciples said, 'Take and eat; this is my Body.'" This follows the Passover meal structure previously outlined, corresponding to the blessing and eating of unleavened bread that took place in the Passover meal. More importantly, Jesus declares the unleavened bread to be his Body and by the power of the Holy Spirit it is made so. This is the first Eucharist and the model by which priests since the time of Jesus have consecrated the unleavened bread in Mass.

Next in the Last Supper (verse 27), the "cup of blessing" is blessed and consumed (also see 1 Corinthians 10:16). This part is the next section in the Passover meal. Much like the bread of the Last Supper differed from the traditional Jewish Passover bread because Jesus made it into his Body, the cup of wine differs from the regular Passover in that Jesus changes it into his Blood. "Then He took a cup, gave thanks, and gave it to them saying, "Drink from it, all of you, for this is my Blood of the covenant, which will be shed on behalf of many for the forgiveness of sins" (Matthew 26:27-28).

Jesus' mention of covenant is also significant. The Last Supper narratives are the only places in the Gospels that Jesus speaks of a covenant. Knowing how significant covenants were in the Old Testament, one should pay close attention to Christ's statement. In the Old Testament, a covenant was sealed by killing a victim whose blood became "the blood of the covenant." In our New Covenant, Jesus "entered once and for all into the sanctuary, not with the blood of goats and calves but with his own blood, thus obtaining eternal redemption" (Hebrews 9:12). **In this way Jesus is the sacrifice of the New Covenant.**

From our look at the Book of Hebrews, we know that the Body and Blood of Christ comprise the seal of the New Covenant (Hebrews 9:12) and must be eaten in order to reach eternal life (John 6:53). The Passover meal that the Jews celebrated each year renewed the covenant established in the original Passover. In the same way, the seal of the New Covenant, the Last Supper, is renewed by its memorial, the Mass. Thus we can see that the Mass is connected to both the Last Supper and the Passover.

Regarding the original Passover meal, remember that in order to save their firstborn from death, families had to consume the sacrificial lamb. When the Passover lamb was brought to the Temple to be sacrificed, it was put on two spits in the form of a cross. This was called **crucifying the lamb**. But where is the unblemished lamb of our New Covenant meal? When we look at the Last Supper, the lamb is noticeably absent. The Apostles would have been looking for a crucified lamb. So where is it? Let's look at some similarities between the Passover lamb (also called Paschal lamb) and Jesus.

Paschal Lamb	**Jesus the Lamb of God**
male without blemish (Exodus 12:5)	male without sin
no broken bones (Exodus 12:46)	although crucified, legs were not broken (John 19:31-36)
sacrificed as substitute for firstborn (Exodus12:12)	sacrificed as substitute for all mankind
after the lamb is offered, it must be eaten (Exodus 12:8)	must be eaten after offering sacrifice (John 6:53)

So Jesus is our Paschal Lamb! As St. Paul says in 1 Corinthians 5:7 "For our paschal Lamb, Christ, has been sacrificed. Therefore, let us celebrate the feast." Christ is also called the Lamb of God in Isaiah 53, John 1:36, and 28 times in the Book of Revelation.

Let's summarize what we know so far about the Last Supper and its association with the Passover meal structure. The beginning of the meal structure is not presented in detail in the Gospels. The rest seems to follow in the proper order. Jesus is the Paschal Lamb, (by the power of the Holy Spirit) the unleavened bread is changed into his Body, and the wine becomes his Blood. Next comes the Great Hallel, the hymn consisting of Psalms 114 to 118, that is referred to in Matthew 26:30. Psalms 116 and 118 are actually being fulfilled in the Paschal mystery of Christ as they are being sung by Jesus and his disciples!

According to the Passover meal structure, the fourth cup should be next. But Matthew 26:30 doesn't say anything about a fourth cup; Jesus and the Apostles went out to the Mount of Olives instead. That is quite odd since the fourth cup was an essential part of the meal. Did He forget about it? No, in fact in Mark 14:25, after drinking the third cup, the "cup of blessing" Jesus tells his Apostles that He won't be drinking any more wine until the day He will "drink it new in the Kingdom of God." So Christ made it quite obvious that He wasn't going to drink a fourth cup of wine at the Last Supper. But why didn't He drink it?

Fourth Cup[36]

Instead of finishing the Passover, Jesus walks over to the garden of Gethsemane on the Mount of Olives to pray. During the Agony in the Garden, Jesus mentions this missing fourth cup in Matthew chapter 26 verses 39 and 42. We can conclude from this passage and elsewhere that the fourth cup deals with Christ's suffering. He is the innocent victim sacrificed for all of mankind's sins.

Leaving the garden, Jesus is arrested and condemned to death. Just before He is nailed to the cross, Jesus is offered wine (Mark 15:23) but refuses to take it. After suffering on the cross, and knowing "everything was now finished," Jesus said, "I thirst!" (John 19:28). In this verse He is calling for the final cup. Then verse 29 of chapter 19 states, "There was a vessel filled with common wine. So they put a sponge soaked in wine on a sprig of hyssop an put it up to His mouth." Hyssop was same the kind of reed or branch used to spread the blood of the Passover lamb (also known as Paschal lamb) on the door frame. Christ's tunic which the soldiers gamble for in John 19:23-24 is the same kind of garment that the high priest wore when offering the Passover sacrifice. And in verse 30, we see "When Jesus had taken the wine, He said, 'It is finished.' And bowing His head, He handed over the spirit." Here He drinks the fourth cup.

Why is this significant? Because this was the last part of the Passover; the meal was not complete without it. So by delaying the fourth cup, He shows that the Passover sacrifice that He began in the upper room at the Last Supper was not complete until the He, the Lamb of God, had been sacrificed on the cross. The drinking of the fourth cup is the last event of Jesus' life that John relates to us in his Gospel. In addition, this whole search for the fourth cup brings forth a significant point about our Mass. The Eucharistic Liturgy does not only make present the Last Supper, it also re-presents Jesus' sacrifice on Golgotha. It is all one piece; the two

---

36. In this section I (again) rely heavily on the work of Dr. Scott Hahn in his many discussions on the fourth cup.

cannot be separated. Or as St. Paul puts it, "For as often as you eat this bread and drink this cup, you proclaim the death of the Lord until He comes" (1 Corinthians 11:26).

Jesus transformed the Passover sacrifice of the Old Covenant into the Eucharistic sacrifice of the New Covenant. We worship God the Father in the way God the Son showed us—in the Eucharistic Liturgy.

The salvation Christ won for us on the cross comes to us especially in the Mass. For in

> "recalling the mysteries of the redemption, [Holy Mother Church] opens up to the faithful the riches of her Lord's powers and merits, so that these are in some way made present for all time; the faithful lay hold of them and are filled with saving grace."[37]

Other Gospel passages relevant to the Mass:
Matthew 5:23 Bringing gifts to the altar
Matthew 8:11 Banquet in the Kingdom
Mark 6:52 They had not understood the loaves
Luke 22:28-30 Eat & drink at table in the Kingdom
Luke 24:13-35 Emmaus: Jesus reads Scripture and explains it (Liturgy
              of the Word) and is made known to them in the break-
              ing of the bread (Liturgy of the Eucharist).
John 13:1-30 Washing of feet and Judas
John 15:1-5 Vine and the branches

Homily

The word "homily" comes from the Greek word for explanation. Appropriately enough, the homily is the sermon in which the priest or deacon explains the day's Bible readings and applies them to the needs of

---

37. *Constitution on the Sacred Liturgy*, art. 102.

the particular congregation. Even before the Mass existed, Jewish synagogue services had commentaries on scripture that were similar to our present day homilies. The homily is an excellent opportunity for instruction on faith and morals. But because of the different needs, ages and backgrounds of the people in the congregation, a good homily is hard to create. So be patient with those priests and deacons who don't give inspiring homilies. God works through them too.

First Homily John Ch.13:31-35; Ch.14-16

Knowing that the Last Supper is the first Mass, it might be appropriate to call Jesus' talks in John chapters 13 through 16 the first homily. Given at the Last Supper, this important discussion touches upon many of the major tenets of the faith: the Father, Christ's own divinity, the Holy Spirit, the paschal mystery, and the Apostles' mission. It may in fact be the most complete look at the Trinity in all of Sacred Scripture. Looking at these chapters of John's Gospel not only gives us theological knowledge but also provides us with an excellent homily, the prototype for all to come.

John 13:31-35

With Judas' departure during the Last Supper meal Jesus' teaching of the Apostles begins. This seems appropriate, for as Judas leaves, only the holy ones remain to hear of their great mission in the kingdom. Jesus first tells them of his own glory and the glory of the Father. Then He, issues a commandment, something that only God can do. "Love one another," is Jesus' simple yet profound command.

What does his command to love one another entail? Initially we might think this to be an easy command to follow but look at what Jesus meant when He spoke of loving one another. In Matthew 5:43-48, Jesus points out that it is easy to love those who love us, for even bad people are nice to their friends. We are called to something much more, we are called to love our enemies and pray for those who persecute us. Have you ever tried to do this? Have you ever really prayed for those who persecute you? It's a radical kind of love. But by loving our enemies we become children of God; growing closer to the Father by loving as He does. And this isn't all we are asked to do.

> "Love is patient, love is kind. It is not jealous, [love] is not pompous, it is not inflated, it is not rude, it does not seek its own interests, it is not quick-tempered, it does not brood over injury, it does not rejoice over wrongdoing but rejoices with the truth. It bears all things, believes all things, hopes all things, endures all things. Love never fails" (1 Corinthians 13:4-8).

All of this is required of us when He says "love one another." Jesus' words so far have been few, but as we can see they are far reaching. Already we have been commanded, not just asked but commanded, to love in a way that suddenly appears very difficult. "This is how all will know that you are my disciples, if you have love for one another" (John 13:35).

John 14

After a brief interruption relating to the prediction of Peter's denial of Jesus, Our Lord again begins to teach the Apostles. "Do not let your hearts be troubled," He says, "You have faith in God; have faith in me." This is a key, for if we have faith as the Apostles have faith, there is nothing to fear. We may live or we may die, either way we will be with the Lord. Jesus shows his Apostles that because they have faith there is a place reserved for each of them in Heaven and informs them (again) He will be going back to the Father. Thomas, who is probably more like us than we would like to admit, asks Jesus how to get there. "I am the way and the truth and the life" (vs. 6) is Jesus' answer. After Philip requests to see the Father, Jesus informs him that "Whoever has seen me has seen the Father," (vs. 9) indicating that Jesus is God (also see John 16:14-15 and 17:10).

"If you love me, you will keep my commandments" (vs. 15). What commandments? Jesus must be speaking of the "love one another" command and also those from the Sermon on the Mount (Matthew chapters 5-7). As for the first, we have already looked at what loving one another entails. Now we see that loving one another is showing love for Jesus. This is why Jesus says (in Matthew 25:40), "Whatever you did for one of these least brothers of mine, you did for me." The reader will already be familiar with some of the commands of the Sermon on the Mount for they are natural extensions of the 10 Commandments (see Matthew 5:21-28 for example). Jesus promises this love for Him through following his words and keeping his commandments will result a manifold return of love from the Father, Son, and Holy Spirit, who will all three dwell with you and in you.

Next, Jesus tells of the Holy Spirit who is to come teaching and reminding them of the truth. Many names and translations of names are given to the Holy Spirit. Take some time to think about how the following relate to the Holy Spirit: paraclete, advocate, counselor, comforter, consoler, protector, defender.

John 15

In the next chapter of the Gospel of John, Jesus continues his explanations with the metaphor: "I am the vine, you are the branches," (15:5). Those who remain in the love of Christ through keeping his commandments (vs. 10) will bear the "fruit" of discipleship while those who don't keep his commandments will be dried up and burned in the fires of hell (vs. 6).

One of the following verses deserves a closer look. Jesus says, "I have told you this so that my joy might be in you and your joy might be complete." This is connected to St. John's first epistle (letter) in which he writes, "We are writing you this so that our joy may be complete," (1 John 1:4). So the question arises, what is it that makes our joy complete? The answer, found in verse 3 of the first chapter of John's first letter, is our joy will be complete when all people are joined in one body, in fellowship with each other, God the Father and Jesus Christ our Lord. At that time, all of God's people will either be in Heaven or headed in the right direction. At that time, our joy will be complete!

Again Jesus states the commandment that we must follow for all of this to happen, "This is my commandment: love one another as I love you." The addition of the ending "as I love you" reminds us of how much He loves us: He died for our sins. This is the very next item Jesus touches upon. "No one has greater love than this, to lay down one's life for one's friends." Here Jesus has taken love to a whole new level. No longer should we hate our enemies and love only our friends and family. Jesus calls us to love our enemies and, if necessary, die for our friends and family. He promises union and life with Him for all those who follow this command. "You are my friends if you do what I command you." "This I command you: love one another."

He tells his Apostles they will be persecuted like He is persecuted. But they know as we know that suffering is part of what we do for friendship and love. They must not worry about worldly things but instead be concerned with being faithful to Christ. What He tells the Apostles is just as applicable to us today as it was to them two thousand years ago. We must reject the many worldly things which bring us to sin and instead seek holiness in Christ. We will "not belong to the world" (vs. 19) but belong to Christ.

John 16

After again reminding his Apostles He is going back to the Father (vs. 5), Jesus says "It is better for you that I go" (vs. 7). But how can this be? Jesus' coming into the world was at this time the definitive point in all of human history! So what could be better about Him being gone? Well, for one thing, everything that the Apostles ask in Jesus name will be done (John 14:13). Also, when Jesus leaves, the Advocate, the Holy Spirit, will come and guide them into all truth (16:12-13). How wonderful the Holy Spirit must be if his presence is better for the Apostles than the continued presence of Christ! All too often we as Catholics neglect to glorify and worship the Holy Spirit. If you are one of the guilty parties, I would suggest you say a little prayer to Him right now.

These few chapters of John's Gospel (13-16) reveal a wealth of information about the Apostles' mission, the Paschal mystery, our redemption and salvation, the new law, and the Father, Son and Holy Spirit.

Profession of Faith (Creed)

All: We believe in one God, the Father, the Almighty, maker of heaven and earth (Genesis 14:19), of all that is seen and unseen (Colossians 1:16). We believe in one Lord, Jesus Christ, the only Son of God, eternally begotten of the Father (Luke 1:35), God from God, Light from Light, true God from true God (John 10:30), begotten, not made, one in Being with the Father (Hebrews 1:3). Through Him all things were made (John 1:1-4). For us men and for our salvation He came down from heaven (John 3:13): (Profound Bow) Notice the profound bow when the Creed speaks of the Incarnation (Jesus coming into the world). A simple bow is bowing the head. In a profound bow one bends at the waist. We make ourselves lower (bow) out of respect for Jesus' action of making Himself lower (Hebrews 2:7) for our sake.

by the power of the Holy Spirit he was born of the Virgin Mary and became man (Matthew 1:18). For our sake he was crucified under Pontius Pilate (John 19:16); he suffered, died, and was buried. On the third day He rose again in fulfillment of the Scriptures (1 Corinthians 15:3); He ascended into heaven (Luke 24:51) and is seated at the right hand of the Father (Luke 22:69; Colossians 3:1). He will come again in glory to judge the living and the dead (2 Tim 4:1), and his kingdom will have no end (Luke 1:33). We believe in the Holy Spirit (Matthew 28:19), the Lord, the giver of life, who proceeds from the Father (John 14:25) and the Son (John 15:26). With the Father and the Son He is worshipped and glorified (John 14:16). He has spoken through the Prophets (1 Pet 1:10-11). We believe in one holy catholic and apostolic Church (Matthew 16:13-19; Matthew 18:18-20; John 17:21; Romans 12:5). We acknowledge one baptism for the forgiveness of sins (Acts 2:38). We look for the resurrection of the dead (Romans 6:5), and the life of the world to come (John 6:54). Amen.

The word "creed" comes from "credo" meaning "I give my heart" or "I believe." So as one would expect, **our Creed outlines the basics of what we believe**. By summarizing the faith of the Church, the Creed also gives us identity, defining who we are. The profession identifies each of us as part of the Catholic Church. **It is our pledge of allegiance**. We commit ourselves to the faith by proclaiming this creed. We, through the Creed, give assent to what we heard in the scripture readings and the homily. God spoke to us through the readings, we now respond to Him through our Profession of Faith.

General Intercessions (Prayer of the Faithful)

Reader: For the needs of the Church: for the pope, the bishops, the shepherds of souls, that they make have renewed vigor to witness to Christ, we pray to the Lord.

All: Lord hear our prayer.

Reader: For an increase in vocations to the priesthood and religious life, we pray to the Lord.

All: Lord hear our prayer.

Reader: For our government leaders, that they promote peace and development of social justice, we pray to the Lord.

All: Lord hear our prayer.

Reader: For the poor, the sick, the persecuted, the imprisoned and all others who are in need of assistance, that God's grace will shine upon them and bring them comfort, we pray to the Lord.

All: Lord hear our prayer.

Reader: For our family members who have died in Christ, that they share in the life and love He promised them, we pray to the Lord.

All: Lord hear our prayer.

At the end, the priest says an extemporaneous concluding prayer.

All: Amen.

What good Father would ignore the holy requests of his children? What groom would ignore the holy requests of his bride? So certainly God, our good Father, and Christ, the perfect Bridegroom, will hear our prayers and answer them by be bringing us to holiness. For if "the fervent prayer of a righteous person is very powerful" (James 5:16), then the Church, the Bride of Christ, is tremendously powerful when in prayer. Since our prayers are truly efficacious, it is fitting that through love we offer "supplications, prayers, petitions, and thanksgivings…for everyone" (1 Tim 2:1-3).

The Prayers of the Faithful follow a well designed format. In them the congregation prays for:

1. needs of the whole Church,
2. public authorities and the salvation of the world,
3. those oppressed by need,
4. and the local community.

This puts us in perspective, for we belong both to the universal Church and to a local church community. We are in the world but not of the world. There is also a time here to offer personal intentions (usually out loud at weekday Mass but silently at the typically larger Sunday Mass). So the Prayers of the Faithful offer both personal participation and community prayer.

> "The celebration of the Mass, the action of Christ and the people of God arrayed hierarchically, is for the Church universal and local as well as for each of the faithful the center of the whole Christian life. In the Mass we have the high point of the work that in Christ God accomplishes to sanctify us and the high point of the worship that the human race offers to the Father, whom we adore through Christ, the Son of God, in the Holy Spirit."[38]

---

38. *General Instruction of the Roman Missal (2000)*, no. 16.

THE LITURGY OF THE EUCHARIST

In some churches, an altar server brings a flame lit from the candle burning next to the lectern and lights two candles near the altar. The candles stand for joy and more importantly for Christ as the light of the world (John 8:12). We imitate Jesus by being a light to the world. As the candles give their whole substance to provide light for others, so we sacrifice, giving our whole being to become light for the world. The shift in focus from word to sacrament can be seen by the accompanying shift in which candles are lit. We have finished the Liturgy of the Word which was prefigured by the synagogue service. Now the Liturgy of the Eucharist begins, where all of the Temple sacrifices are fulfilled in the sacrifice of Jesus.

Rite of Preparation

Notice the altar servers' diligent preparation of the altar. It is similar to the Apostles' preparation for the Last Supper (Matthew 28:19-20). The chalice (gold cup) is placed on the altar along with the paten (gold plate). These containers we use to hold the Body and Blood of Christ show our faith in Christ's Presence. That is why the chalice and paten are made of gold and are often ornate. The purificator and corporal (both are small cloths) are also placed on the altar. Instead of using the Lectionary, the priest will make use of a book called the Sacramentary for the remainder of Mass.

Procession of the Gifts

At the same time the altar is being prepared, an offertory song is sung and a collection is taken. In the early days of Christianity, the people brought all kinds of things: flowers, chickens, geese, oil, honey, clothes, shoes, bread, wine, and other gifts for the poor, the priest, and the celebration of the Mass. Things got messy! Now we simply give money. But be generous, for "God loves the cheerful giver" (2 Corinthians 9:7) and the money you give goes to the poor and to the needs of the Church. By giving to the needy (Matthew 25:40) and the Church (Acts 9:4) you are giving help to Christ Himself.

Following the preparation of the altar, the procession of the gifts can take place. In the same way the first half of Mass began with the entrance procession, the beginning of the second half, the Liturgy of the Eucharist, is clearly distinguished by the procession of gifts. At this time the gifts of bread and wine are brought to the altar by members of the congregation along with any monetary offering. The bread is on a paten (gold plate) and the wine and water are in cruets (little bottles).

The Jewish Temple was designed to look like Heaven, the sanctuaries of the Jewish synagogues represented Heaven, and much of the architecture we as Catholics have used for centuries in our churches comes from our Jewish ancestors. It's no surprise, then, that our sanctuaries represent Heaven. In the raised front part (sanctuary) of church buildings, especially older ones, we often find heavenly scenes with angels and saints painted on the ceilings. The choir is often positioned in a loft so their singing seems to be coming from choirs of angels in Heaven. The nave of the church, where the congregation sits, represents the Church on earth. There are often earthly scenes painted in this area or pictures of saints who provide an example of how to live here on earth. Now that the layout of the church building is understood, the procession of the gifts has a whole new meaning. The people (representing us) who come forward from the congregation to bring the gifts to the sanctuary are bringing our gifts to Heaven!

But our gifts of bread, wine, and money seem like insignificant gifts to bring to Heaven. It would seem more appropriate to imitate the Magi who brought precious gifts of gold, frankincense, and myrrh to our Savior (Matthew 2:11). In fact, we wouldn't even have these gifts if God hadn't given them to us, so aren't we just giving Him what is already his? Yes, but giving something back to God is the very definition of sacrifice. We are offering little sacrifices to God.

But we can do much more. Remember before Mass when you prayed about the good things and the bad things that you did since your last Mass? In the Penitential Rite, the bad things (venial sins) were eliminated. Here in the procession of gifts we use the good things. In the same way the bread and wine are really gifts from God that we give back to God, so are our good deeds. For we can accomplish nothing without the grace of God. Only with his aid are we empowered to do good. Yet these good deeds are all we have to give. So, take all of your kind words, all of your smiles, all of your good deeds and everything that you have done for the Lord, and tie them up in a little package. Put a ribbon around it and a bow on top and present the gift of your life to the Lord along with the gifts of bread and wine that are brought forth to the altar. For even these gifts of bread, wine, and money represent our lives because, "in faith, any gift is a gift of self, because the believer can never separate himself from what he is offering."[39] In other words, when you put ten dollars in the collection, you could have spent this money on yourself, but instead you sacrificed by giving some of your own life to God.

Take all of your gifts to God, physical and spiritual, and place them on the altar. Everything we have goes on the altar to be made holy in Christ. He who will take the insignificant gifts of bread and wine and transform them into the most valuable gifts in the whole world, his Body and Blood, will also through the Eucharist transform your gift of self!

---

39. Von Spyer. *Holy Mass.* Ignatius, p. 55.

How will you be transformed? By becoming more and more like God. You have already taken a step in the right direction by doing what God does best, giving. Our offering of bread and wine becomes Christ's offering of his Body and Blood to the Father. Only these gifts from God (bread and wine) are gifts that become God (Jesus' Body and Blood). Yet, in this procession, we join our gifts, our own imperfect lives, to Christ's perfect offering to the Father. By uniting our sacrificial offerings (little sacrifices) to Christ's one true sacrifice, we open the doors to our hearts. Then Christ, seeing the open door to your heart, comes and fills your soul with grace, that is, his own divine life. This happens primarily through reception of Jesus' Body and Blood at Mass. It transforms your life to make you more like Jesus who for all eternity offers his life to the Father.

It should now be easy to see that the procession of the gifts reflects our journey to Heaven. We come out from the world (represented by nave) to the threshold of Heaven (represented by altar) to present the gift of our lives (Romans 12:1), united with Christ's self-offering (represented by bread and wine), to God the Father (represented by priest) in Heaven (represented by sanctuary). If we are found acceptable, God forms us into partakers in the divine nature (2 Pet 1:4).

We are approaching Heaven's worship of God. It is time to prepare our hearts for the climax of this great mystery.

Preparation of the Gifts

Priest: Blessed are you Lord God of all creation. Through your goodness we have this bread to offer, which earth has given and human hands have made (from Jewish Passover meal). It will become for us the bread of life (John 6:35).

Remember the loaves of bread that Jesus multiplied to feed the crowd (John 6:9-11)? If the boy's little gift was changed by Jesus into such a large quantity, then Jesus will certainly receive our little gifts and change them into plenty of food for our souls (grace). If the boy's small offering can through the power of Christ feed the multitude, then our bread which is offered through Jesus and actually becomes Jesus will do much, much more. Surely it will fill the soul of every grace-starved person. Surely it will bring everlasting life (John 6:51)!

On Holy Thursday night, members of the Temple went out to the Kidron Valley where Jesus was arrested and gave 30 silver pieces, the same amount Judas was given to betray Jesus (Matthew 26:15 and 27:3), for barley which they tied just as they tied Jesus' hands when he was arrested. On the next day (the day Christ was killed) the barley sheaf was cut. This was done when Christ was arrested in the garden. They brought the sheaves of barley across the same bridge they brought Christ and into the Temple. A Temple priest put his hands over the barley and puts the sins of the community on it. Temple servants thrashed the barley with rods until the grain separated from chaff (stalks) just as they scourged Christ. This barley was made into bread while Jesus made Himself the Bread of life.[40]

Priest whispers: By the mingling of this water and wine may we come to share in the divinity of Christ who humbled Himself to share in our humanity.

See how the wine is mingled with a little water? The water represents humanity while the wine symbolizes divinity. Jesus assumed human nature, sharing in our humanity. Now we (represented by water) hope to some day share in his divinity, represented here by wine. So the Son of God became the Son of Man so the sons of men could become sons of God. More clearly, Jesus became man and died on the cross so we could know and love God and become his children. Once the water and wine are mingled, they become one inseparable substance. Likewise, once we are joined with Christ in Heaven, we will never be separated from Him again.

On a practical level, the custom of putting water in the wine came from the Greco-Roman world where wine was very strong and decent folks only

---

40. Preceding paragraph is adapted from Fr. James Meagher's *How Christ Said the First Mass.* Tan, p 199-202.

drank wine that had been mixed with water. The wine and water also remind us of the blood and water flowing from Christ's side as He hung on the cross (John 19:34).

Priest: Blessed are you, Lord, God of all creation. Through your goodness we have this wine to offer, fruit of the vine and work of human hands (from Jewish Passover meal). It will become our spiritual drink (Luke 22:17-18).

All: Blessed be God for ever (Ps 68:36).

Even though much has been said about our self-offering, it is important to remember that Christ's self-offering is by far the most important action in the Mass. Historically this took place when He shed his blood on the cross. Eternally this takes place as Christ offers Himself in Heaven to the Father. The Mass makes this sacrifice present to us today as the bread becomes his Body and the wine becomes his Blood.

Priest: Lord God, we ask you to receive us and be pleased with the sacrifice we offer you with humble and contrite hearts (Dan 3:39-40).

This short prayer has three important points. First, as mentioned previously, the Lord receives not only our gifts but also us. Second, we help offer the sacrifice in Mass. Third, we offer this sacrifice with humility.

The first of these points has already been explored in some detail. The second, though, deserves additional attention. The fact that we offer sacrifice brings to light an important truth, namely, that **we are priests** (see Rev 5:10 & 1 Peter 2:5). As noted earlier, everyone who offers sacrifice to God is by definition a priest. The essence of priesthood is sacrifice. But this seems strange to most Catholics. A little explanation will help. The men we call priests are as you might guess a different type of priest, ordained clergymen, part of the ministerial priesthood, while we on the other hand are part of the royal priesthood of the believers (laity). The ordained priests stand in the place of Christ offering here before our eyes the same sacrifice that Jesus offers eternally in Heaven. The priestly congregation, however, offers a different sacrifice. "[T]hey give thanks to the Father and offer the victim not only through the hands of the priest but also together with him and learn to offer themselves."[41] Stated another way, the people of God do in a certain way assist the priest in offering Christ's sacrifice and also offer their own sacrifice of self. Just as Jesus' total self-offering in Heaven is a sacrifice, our own offering of self is sacrificial. Throughout the Mass one should keep in mind that the principle act of Christ is his offering of self to the Father and that our principle act is a self-offering that images (imperfectly) Christ's gift.

The third point, which is about how we sacrifice, is small but nevertheless important. Psalm 51 reminds us that God wants "a contrite spirit. A humbled, contrite heart [He] will not spurn." Likewise, we must offer **sacrifice with humility**. Yet humility is quite possibly the most neglected virtue of our time. We seem all too absorbed with instilling self confidence and providing assertiveness training. Humility has gone out the window. Because it requires us to look beyond ourselves to the needs of others, it is the key virtue in self-offering. I am the humblest person in the whole world. ☺ How humble are you?

The Church sums up the effect of these offerings nicely as she notes,

> "on the one hand, the Church, united with her Lord and 'in the Holy Spirit,' blesses the Father 'for his inexpressible gift' in her adoration, praise, and thanksgiving. On the other hand, until the consummation of God's plan, the Church never ceases to present to the Father the offering of his own gifts and to beg him to send the Holy Spirit upon that offering, upon herself, upon the faithful, and upon the whole world, so that through communion in the death and resurrection of Christ the Priest, and by the power of the Spirit, these divine blessings will bring forth the fruits of life 'to the praise of his glorious grace.'"[42]

---

41. *General Instruction of the Roman Missal (2000)*, no. 95.
42. *Catechism of the Catholic Church*, par. 1083.

Priest whispers: Lord wash away my iniquity, cleanse me from all my sin (Ps 51:1-4).

The priest washes his hands not to cleanse them from dirt but to cleanse him from sin. This baptism-type washing, called the Lavabo, comes to us from an ancient Jewish custom. It was necessary in the early Church because after the priest received animals, food, clothing, etceteras, as offertory gifts, his hands were in need of a good washing.

Prayer Over the Gifts

Priest: Pray brethren, that our sacrifice may be acceptable to God, the almighty Father (Hebrews 12:28).

All: May the Lord accept the sacrifice at your hands for the praise and glory of his name, for our good and the good of all his Church (Ps 50:23).

Priest: Lord, may the bread and cup we offer bring your Church the unity and peace they signify. We ask this in the name of Jesus the Lord. All: Amen.

The old Latin text for this part of the Mass states, "Pray brethren, that your sacrifice and mine may be acceptable..." Unlike our present wording which only mentions one sacrifice, the Latin text shows both the sacrifice of Christ and the sacrifice of our lives. One may ask why we call our self-giving a sacrifice if Jesus' sacrifice is the only true sacrifice. But it is clear that while Jesus is the only true Son of God, we are still adopted sons and daughters of God in the Son. In a similar way, Jesus' sacrifice is the only true sacrifice and our sacrifices are merely imitations joining us to his eternal sacrifice. The introduction to the General Instruction of the Roman Missal points this out in the statement, "Through the ministry of priests, the people's spiritual sacrifice is brought to completeness in union with the sacrifice of Christ, our one and only Mediator."[43]

---

43. *General Instruction of the Roman Missal (2000)*, no. 5.

Jesus' sacrifice is different from our own even in basic purpose and character. His sacrifice could be termed the true sacrifice and ours called spiritual sacrifices. This would be in line with St. Peters' call to "like living stones, let yourself be built into a spiritual house to be a holy priesthood to **offer spiritual sacrifices** acceptable to God through Jesus Christ" (1 Peter 2:5; Romans 12:1). It is possible that because of sin the sacrifice of our lives, our offering, may be found unacceptable. The sacrifice of Christ in the Mass, on the other hand, is the perfect sacrifice and the Father will always accept it throughout all of eternity. Thus even if we're sinful and the priest is no good, the Mass itself is always accepted by the Father because Christ is the true priest offering the perfect sacrifice of his own life.

Eucharistic Prayer

The climax of the whole Mass is the Eucharistic Prayer.[44] In this prayer the Church gives thanks to God for the whole work of salvation. There are four main Eucharistic Prayers that the priest may choose from when celebrating a regular Mass. There are additional Eucharistic prayers for Masses with children and reconciliation. They are all addressed to God the Father and the priest may select whichever one he feels is appropriate for the occasion. Keep in mind that the Mass is not primarily a prayer to Jesus but a prayer of Jesus and his Church to the Father. Worship of the Eucharist is "directed towards God the Father through Jesus Christ in the Holy Spirit."[45]

---

44. *General Instruction of the Roman Missal (2000)*, no. 30.
45. John Paul II. *The Mystery and Worship of the Eucharist*, 3.

Introductory Dialogue

Priest: The Lord be with you (used in todah offering, p.47).
All: And also with you.
Priest: Lift up your hearts. (Sursum Corda)
All: We lift them up to the Lord (Lam 3:41).
Priest: Let us give thanks to the Lord our God (Colossians 3:17).
All: It is right to give Him thanks and praise (Colossians 1:3).

The priest's "Lift up your hearts" is **our invitation into Heaven**. With our acceptance ("We lift them up to the Lord") of the invite we move into heavenly worship. So the Lord is with us and we are now with Him. Heaven and earth are united here at the altar! Instead of our eyes, we lift up our hearts because we will be walking in faith and our eyes may soon deceive us (see 2 Corinthians 5:7). We must look with hearts of faith on what appears to be bread and see Jesus present in the Eucharist. Further, it may look like we are merely worshipping here on earth but in actuality we are mysteriously joined with Heaven.

Preface

Priest: Father, it is our duty and our salvation, always and everywhere to give you thanks through your beloved Son, Jesus Christ. He is the Word through whom you made the universe, the Savior you sent to redeem us. By the power of the Holy Spirit he took flesh and was born of the Virgin Mary. For our sake he opened his arms on the cross; he put an end to death and revealed the resurrection. In this He fulfilled your will and won for You a holy people. And so we join the angels and the saints in proclaiming you glory as we say:

The Preface provides a transition into the heart of the Eucharistic Prayer. Here we enter into an area so vital to proper celebration of the Mass that it has been used with very little change since the early days of the Church.

Even in the earliest days of Christianity, Mass was considered both a remembrance of the sacrifice of Christ and also a festive thanksgiving (eucharistia) meal. It was then and still is now the center of Christian worship. Outlined here are a few of the many references to the Mass found in writings of the early Christian Church.

Among the earliest known Christian writings outside of the New Testament is the *Teaching of the Twelve Apostles* (Didache ton Dodeka Apostolon) composed in about 80 A.D. Known as the *Didache*, or *Teaching*, this writing reminds the early Christians that only the baptized (9) can assemble for the Eucharist. It also states "On the Lord's own day, assemble in common to break bread and offer thanks; but first confess your sins so that your sacrifice may be pure (14)."[46]

Similar sentiments are expressed in a more detailed outline by St. Justin Martyr in his letter explaining the Eucharistic celebration to emperor Antoninus Pius. Although the Mass has gone through many changes since that time, the basic format of the Eucharistic celebration that St. Justin described in the year 155 A.D. is the same as ours today.

St. Justin Martyr's Description[47]	*My Comments*
On the day we call the day of the sun, all who dwell in the city or country gather in the same place.	St. Justin states that all the people came together on Sunday (Acts 20:7; 1 Corinthians 16:2). We do the same.
The memoirs of the Apostles and the writings of the prophets are read, as much as time permits.	The memoirs of the Apostles are the books of the New Testament and the writings of the prophets are part of the Old Testament. These are our readings at Mass.
When the reader has finished, he who presides over those gathered admonishes and challenges them to imitate these beautiful things.	This is a description of the homily given by the presiding priest.

46. Harden. *Treasury of Catholic Wisdom.* Ignatius, pp. 5-8.
47. *Catechism of the Catholic Church*, par. 1345.

Then we all rise together and offer prayers for ourselves…and for all others, wherever they may be found righteous by our life and actions, and faithful to the commandments, so as to obtain eternal salvation.

These are the general intercessions, also called the prayers of the faithful.

When the prayers are concluded we exchange the kiss.

Instead of the kiss of peace, we in the United States shake hands as a sign of peace.

Then someone brings bread and a cup of water and wine mixed together to him who presides over the brethren.

This is the Presentation of the Gifts. Someone from the congregation brings the gifts of bread, wine, and water to the priest.

He takes them and offers praise and glory to the Father of the universe, through the name of the Son and the Holy Spirit and for a considerable time he gives thanks (in Greek: eucharistia) that we have been judged worthy of these gifts.

This is comparable to the Eucharistic Prayer.

When he has concluded the prayers and thanksgivings, all present give voice to an acclamation by saying: 'Amen.'

This is the Great Amen.

When he who presides has given thanks and the people have responded, those whom we call deacons give to those present the "eucharisted" bread, wine and water and take them to those who are absent.

Although priests and deacons are the primary ones responsible for distribution of communion, this responsibility can occasionally be delegated to lay people if serious need demands it.

Writing in about the year 200A.D., St. Irenaeus of Lyons says:

> "Sacrifice as such has not been reprobated. There were sacrifices then, sacrifices among the people; and there are sacrifices now, sacrifices in the Church. Only the kind has been changed; for now the sacrifice is offered not by slaves but by free men."

> "For thanksgiving is consistent with our opinion; and the Eucharist confirms our opinion. For we offer to Him those things which are His, declaring in a fit manner the gift and the acceptance of flesh and spirit. For as the bread from the earth, receiving invocation of God, is no longer common bread but the Eucharist, consisting of two elements, earthly and heavenly, so also our bodies, when they receive the Eucharist, are no longer corruptible but have the hope of resurrection into eternity."

> "Only the Catholic Church can offer to God the sacrifice which is pleasing to him, announced by the prophets, namely the sacrifice of the Eucharist. It utilizes the products of creation, bread, and wine…These elements are consecrated by the Church by the words of Christ as handed down in tradition."[48]

St. Athanasius who lived from 296-373 A.D. reminds us "it is not a temporal feast that we come to, but an eternal, heavenly feast!"[49]

Holy, Holy, Holy

All: Holy, holy, holy Lord, God of power and might (Is 6:3; Rev 4:8). Heaven and earth are full of your glory (Romans 1:19-20). Hosanna in the highest (Mk 11:10). Blessed is he who comes in the name of the Lord (Ps 118:26; Luke 13:35 and 19:38). Hosanna in the highest (Matthew 21:9; Mk 11:9-10)!

---

48. Jurgens. *Faith of the Early Fathers* (Volume 1). Liturgical, p. 95-96.
49. *Epistolae Festales*, 4,3.

We join with the angels and saints in singing of the glory of God! This song of praise is also called the Sanctus, Acclamation, or Trisagion ("Tris" = three, "agion" = holy). The Old Testament was written in the Hebrew language which had no superlative. In order to say pretti*est* or smart*est* or fast*est*, the word had to be repeated three times. To say something is very holy one would say "holy, holy." This is why the place where the Ark of the Covenant was kept was called the Holy of Holies. To indicate the superlative "holi*est*" one would say "holy, holy, holy." Therefore the song indicates that the Lord is absolutely the holiest one of all. The word "hosanna" means "God saves" and as such has a strong connection to the name Jesus which also means "God saves" (see Matthew 1:21).

Eucharistic Prayer II

Epiclesis

Priest: Lord you are holy indeed, the fountain of all holiness (2 Maccabees 14:36). Let your Spirit come upon these gifts to make them holy, so that they may become for us the body and blood of our Lord, Jesus Christ (John 6)

The Epiclesis is also called "the invocation" since in it we invoke or call on the Holy Spirit to come down and bless the gifts. The priest extends his hands while saying the words and traces the sign of the cross above the gifts. Bells are sometimes rung here at the Epiclesis and later at the Consecration to get the attention of the congregation so they will be sure to pay attention during these most important parts of the Mass. This was necessary when the Mass was in Latin since many people didn't understand Latin and were confused about what went on in the Mass. These members of the congregation often prayed rosaries or other private devotions. Now Mass is usually celebrated English, so there is no excuse for a lack of participation. Because the Holy Mass is the highest form of prayer in the Church, other devotions should not keep our attention during the Eucharistic celebration.

The Mass is the highest prayer that the Church possesses because it re-presents Jesus' self-offering to the Father for us. Although when Jesus' sacrifice is mentioned, we most often think of the cross, Christ's whole life is salvational (Matthew 8:16-17). Because the Mass makes present the redemption that Christ won, it parallels Jesus' life.

Part of Mass	*Jesus' Life*
Entrance Song announces the beginning of Mass.	Gabriel's announcement (Luke 1:26-38) and Mary's Magnificat (Luke 1:46-56) announce the beginning of Christ's life.
Entrance Procession priest and servers go to proper place so that Mass can begin.	Mary and Joseph go to Bethlehem, the proper place for Jesus to beborn (Luke 2:1-7).
Penitential Rite people of God repent of their sins so the Bride (Church) is pure for the coming of the Groom (Christ).	John the Baptist (Mk 1:4-6) preaches repentance to Israel, the people of God, so they will be pure for the coming of the Messiah (Christ).
Gloria Congregation thanks the Lord for making them pure. They sing "Glory to God in the highest and peace to his people on earth."	In thanksgiving to the Lord for sending his Son into the world so that we might be made pure and reach everlasting life, the angels at Jesus' birth sing, "Glory to God in the highest and peace to his people on earth" (Luke 2:14).

First & Second Readings

As the Old and New Testament scriptures are read, we begin to grow in our knowledge of God. Without the Gospels, however, we don't get a clear, full picture of Jesus.

The first two readings are analogous to the time that the Jews spent waiting for the Messiah and the time of Jesus' hidden life.

His "hidden life" is the early part of his life which the Gospels do not relate in any detail.

Gospel

Here the word of God reveals Jesus' life in the fullest way.

The Eternal Word (John 1:14), Jesus Christ, comes to us in public ministry, revealing himself in the fullest way.

Procession of the Gifts, Holy, Holy, Holy

Gifts are brought forward to become the sacrifice.

They will be transformed (transubstantiated) into Jesus, the perfect sacrifice. After prayer, the congregation says, "Hosanna in the highest. Blessed is he who comes in the name of the Lord. Hosanna in the highest."

This is comparable to Jesus' final entrance into Jerusalem (Matthew 21:1-11, Mark 11:1-11, Luke 19:28-40). Here Jesus can be seen as the perfect gift coming forward to Jerusalem to be sacrificed for our sins. Jerusalem (and particularly the Temple) was, in the Jewish mindset, the place where sacrifice should take place.

While entering the city, the crowds shouted, "Hosanna to the Son of David; blessed is he who comes in the name of the Lord; hosanna in the highest" (Matthew 21:9).

Epiclesis

The Holy Spirit comes upon our gifts to make them holy, so they will become the Body and Blood of Jesus.

At Jesus' Baptism (Mt 3:13-16; Mk 1:9-11; Lk 3:21-22; 4:14-19), the Holy Spirit comes upon Him and anoints Him to launch his public ministry.

Narrative of Institution
The priest relates Jesus'
words at the Last Supper.

Jesus speaks at the Last Supper.

Elevation
The host (Latin for victim)
is lifted up and calls us to unity
through receiving Jesus.

Jesus is lifted up on the cross so that
all people may come together in
Him (Jn12:32).

Our Father
The Lord's Prayer is
recited in Mass.

Jesus teaches his disciples to pray by
giving them the Our Father
(Matthew 6:9-15; Luke 11:2-4).

Fraction Rite
We see Jesus, present in the
Eucharist, being broken anew
as the Lamb of God is offered
for our salvation.

While fulfilling his role as the Lamb
of God who takes away the sins of
the world, Jesus is broken (dies) on
the cross.

Commingling
The Body and Blood
of Jesus are united as a small piece
of Host is dropped in the chalice.

The Body and Soul of Jesus are
reunited at his Resurrection.

Communion
We are intimately united to
Jesus through reception
of his Body and Blood.

At the Last Supper the Apostles are
intimately united to Jesus through
reception of his Body and Blood.

Dismissal
The priest (standing in the person
of Christ) asks the people to
"Go in peace to love and
serve the Lord."

Jesus asks his Apostles to
"Go…make disciples of all nations,
baptizing them…"
(Matthew 28:19).

Narrative of Institution

Consecration

Before He was given up to death (Phil 2:8), a death he freely accepted (John 10:17-18), He took bread and gave you thanks. He broke the bread, gave it to his disciples, and said: Take this, all of you, and eat it: this is my Body which will be given up for you (Matthew 26:26-28; Mark 14:22-24; 1 Corinthians 11:23-26).

All (silently): My Lord and my God! (John 20:28-29)

When supper was ended, he took the cup. Again He gave you thanks and praise, gave the cup to his disciples, and said: Take this, all of you, and drink from it: this is the cup of my blood, the blood of the new and everlasting covenant (Hebrews 13:20). It will be shed for you and for all so that sins may be forgiven.

Remembrance

Do this in memory of me (Matthew 26:26-28; Mark 14:22-24; 1 Corinthians 11:23-26).

All (silently): My Lord and my God! (John 20:28-29)

Priest: Let us proclaim the mystery of faith.

Memorial Acclamation

All: Dying you destroyed our death, rising you restored our life, Lord Jesus come in glory (Hebrews 2:14-15).

Though we call this part of the Mass the "Narrative of Institution," using the word "Narrative" to describe what is happening here is weak. **We are not just hearing the Last Supper read to us, we are participating in it!** At our Mass the priest not only tells us what happened at the Last Supper, he also makes that sacred meal truly present in our midst. When we participate in the Eucharistic celebration the graces of the paschal mystery (Christ's passion, death and resurrection) fill our souls.

Mass is the primary way Christ stays present in the Church. It is true that God is omnipresent (present everywhere) but his presence in the Mass goes above and beyond this. He is present in the congregation which makes up his body. He is present in the priest since Christ is the High Priest. He is present in God's word read to us from scripture since He is the Eternal Word. He is present in the fullest sense when the bread and wine become his Body and Blood. This presence is unsurpassed.[50]

The Consecration, where the bread and wine are changed into the Body and Blood of Christ, is the pinnacle of the entire Mass. This change from bread into Body and wine into Blood is called transubstantiation. The word seems intimidating at first but it simply means a change (trans) of substance (substanti). In our particular case, it refers to the miraculous change of ordinary bread and wine into Jesus Himself. Just think, now all your friends will think you are really smart when you speak of the miracle of transubstantiation.

The Church had always believed that Christ is present in the Eucharist, but the early Church councils didn't provide any detailed explanation of this mystery. Consequently, the formal definition of transubstantiation at the Fourth Lateran Council resulted in so much awe for the Eucharist that many people stopped receiving the Sacrament altogether (theologians were not pleased with this result). Consequently the Church required the people to receive the Eucharist at least once a year. The Fourth Lateran Council in 1215 proclaimed the following regarding this mystery:

> "Jesus Christ is both priest and sacrifice. In the Sacrament of the Altar, under the species of bread and wine, His Body and Blood are truly contained, the bread having been transubstantiated into this Body and the wine into His Blood by the divine power. In

---

50. Adapted from *Constitution on the Sacred Liturgy*, art. 7.

order to complete the mystery of unity, we receive from Him what He received from us. And no one is able to confect this Sacrament except the priest who is properly ordained according to the keys of the Church, which Jesus Christ Himself gave to the Apostles and their successors."[51]

This excerpt brings up another important point. Jesus is both priest and victim of the holy Sacrifice of the Mass. The principal priest in every Mass is of course Jesus Christ, who offers his Body and Blood to the Father, through the human priest. Further, we know that Jesus is the true sacrifice of the Mass. His self-offering on the cross becomes present at the Mass. At the consecration, we see Christ (present under the appearance of bread) on the cross (represented by altar). As the Old Covenants were sealed with the blood of animals so the New Covenant is sealed with the Blood of Christ. The Mass itself, because of its unity with the Blood of Christ, is the seal and the perpetual renewal of the New Covenant.

Covenants always involve an mutual exchange of persons and yield sacred kinship. The Mass is covenant related because in it Jesus gives Himself to us and asks us to give ourselves to Him. All who join themselves with Christ become part of God's Family, the mystical body of Christ. Thus in this memorial of Christ's love for us, his Blood bonds us together as his family.

Since God is present as the priest elevates the Host (which means "victim"), we have an opportunity for adoration. In the same way that the faithful adore Christ in a monstrance or tabernacle, the elevation of the Host provides a short opportunity to adore the Lord. Don't miss your chance! Here at the elevation we get a little taste of the Beatific Vision!

Let's look at the what the saints have to say about the Eucharist and the Mass.

---

51. Guernsey. *Adoration*. Ignatius, p. 61.

St. Cyril (315 A.D. to 386 A.D.) of Jerusalem writes:

"Do not, therefore, regard the Bread and the Wine as simply that; for they are, according to the Master's declaration, the Body and Blood of Christ. Even though the senses suggest to you the other, let faith make you firm. Do not judge in this matter by taste, but—be fully assured by the faith, not doubting that you have been deemed worthy of the Body and Blood of Christ."[52]

St. Justin states:

"Just as through the Word of God Jesus Christ became incarnate, took flesh and blood for our salvation, in the same way this food, which has become Eucharist thanks to the prayer formed out of the words of Christ, and which nourishes and is assimilated into our flesh and blood, is the flesh and blood of incarnate Jesus: this is the doctrine that we have received."[53]

See also St. Philip Neri's love for the Eucharist:

"So enraptured did he become when offering the Holy Sacrifice that it became the practice for those who attended his Mass to retire at the Agnus Dei. Even the server would leave the chapel after extinguishing the candles, lighting a little lamp and placing outside the door a notice to give warning that the Father was saying Mass. Two hours later he would return, relight the candles and the Mass would be continued."[54]

That seems like a long time until you find out St. Dominic Savio knelt before the Blessed Sacrament for more than six hours every day.[55]

---

52. Jurgens. *Faith of the Early Fathers* (Volume 1). Liturgical, p. 361.
53. Deiss. *It's the Lord's Supper.* Paulist, p. 27.
54. Butler's *Lives of the Saints* (Volume II). Pp. 398-399.
55. Kaczmarek. *Hidden Treasure.* Trinity, p. 21.

Observe the love for the Mass that St. John Vianney displays in his simple yet profound words:

> "All good works together are not of equal value with the sacrifice of the Mass, because they are the works of men, and the holy Mass is the work of God. Martyrdom is nothing in comparison; it is the sacrifice that man makes of his life to God; the Mass is the sacrifice that God makes to man of His Body and of His Blood…After the Consecration, when I hold in my hands the most holy Body of Our Lord, and when I am in discouragement, seeing myself worthy of nothing but Hell, I say to myself, "Ah, if I could at least take Him with me! Hell would be sweet with Him; I could be content to remain suffering there for all eternity, if we were together. But then there would be no more Hell; the flames of love would extinguish those of justice…. How beautiful it is. After the Consecration, the good God is there as He is in Heaven. If man well understood this mystery, he would die of love…If someone said to us, 'At such an hour a dead person is to be raised to life,' we should run very quickly to see it. But is not the Consecration, which changes bread and wine into the Body and Blood of God, a much greater miracle than to raise a person to life?"[56]

Remember that it is not this mystery that must come down to our everyday life, but our everyday life that must be raised up to enter the Mystery of Faith. Every day we should, like the saints, strive to grow in our understanding of the Eucharist.

Two small but significant parts follow the consecration. In the remembrance (Anamnesis or memorial), we hear Jesus' command to do this (the New Passover) in remembrance of Him. Notice he does not say just read this in remembrance of Him. No, He asks us to do it. In the Hebrew mindset, remembrance means re-presentation. It is both a proclamation

---

56. Vianney. *The Little Catechism of the Cure of Ars.* Tan, pp. 37-38.

and participation. Therefore, the offering that Christ made at the Last Supper clearly happens in the present at the Mass. The second part is the Memorial Acclamation. Depending on liturgical seasons, feast days, and similar concerns, the priest will choose from one of the approved acclamations.

Offering and Intercessions

Priest: In memory of his death and resurrection, we offer You, Father, this life-giving bread, this saving cup (John 6:51). We thank you for counting us worthy to stand in your presence and serve you (Anaphora of Hippolytus 215A.D.). May all of us who share in the Body and Blood of Christ be brought together in unity by the Holy Spirit (1 Corinthians 10:17). Lord, remember your Church throughout the world; make us grow in love, together with N. our Pope, N. our bishop, and all the clergy. Remember our brothers and sisters who have gone to their rest in the hope of rising again (2 Maccabees 12:45-46); bring them and all the departed into the light of your presence. Have mercy on us all; make us worthy to share eternal life with Mary, the virgin Mother of God, with the apostles, and with all the saints who have done your will throughout the ages. May we praise you in union with them, and give glory through your Son, Jesus Christ (2 Thessalonians 1:4-5).

Dissecting this prayer into its parts will remind us of several important issues. The phrase "*we offer You, Father, this life-giving bread, this saving cup*" reminds us that in a some way, we are part of a lay priesthood that participates in the offering of the Mass. The following "*We thank you for counting us worthy to stand in your presence*" reminds us that we are in God's presence, united to Heaven during the Mass. The section saying "*all of us who share in the Body and Blood of Christ be brought together in unity*" reminds us that eating the Body of Christ (Eucharist) makes us the mystical body of Christ (Church). Or to say this another way, Communion builds community. The mention of the other members of the mystical body makes it clear that the Eucharist is celebrated in union with the whole Church of all places and all times, living and dead, who share in the redemption and salvation Christ offers. We unite our praise with theirs, glorifying the Father through the Son.

> "[T]he Eucharistic Mystery stands at the heart and center of the liturgy, since it is the font of life by which we are cleansed and strengthened to live not for ourselves but for God, and to be united in love among ourselves."[57]

Final Doxology

Through Him, with Him, in Him, in the unity of the Holy Spirit, all glory and honor is yours almighty Father, for ever and ever (Romans 11:36).
The Doxology (meaning "word of glory") sounds like the Glory Be:

> Glory be to the Father, and to the Son, and to the Holy Spirit as it was in the beginning, is now, and ever shall be, world without end. Amen.

But there is a problem: Where does the glory go? In the Doxology it says "all glory and honor are yours almighty Father" while the Glory Be says the glory goes to the Father and Son and Holy Spirit. Is there a contradiction between the Mass and a classic Catholic prayer? Does the glory go only to the Father or to all three persons of the Trinity?

It is proper for us to give praise and glory to any of the three. That is how the Glory Be states it, "Glory be to the Father and to the Son and to the Holy Spirit." Most of the attention, however, centers around Jesus since he is the most easily recognizable of the three. But instead of taking all the glory for Himself, Jesus instead says in essence, "I owe it all to my Father." The key to this whole puzzle, then, is in the first phrase of the Doxology, "Through Him, with Him, in Him." Who is Him? Jesus. We are no longer talking about bread. It is now Him, that is, Jesus. All glory and honor go to the Father, through Jesus.

---

57. Paul VI. *Mystery of Faith*. St. Paul, p. 5.

Jesus, though He gets the glory from us, gives it to his heavenly Father (John 14:13). He returns the life and love that the Father gave Him. But let's not forget the Holy Spirit. What about Him? All is done in the unity of the Holy Spirit. Jesus works in union with the Holy Spirit in giving glory to the Father. Thus in all this action we can see the basic format of every good prayer: the goal is the Father, the way is the Son, the power is the Holy Spirit. Or as Pope John Paul II put it,

> "This worship is directed towards God the Father through Jesus Christ in the Holy Spirit...It is also directed, in the Holy Spirit, to the incarnate Son, in the economy of salvation, especially at that moment of supreme dedication and total abandonment of Himself to which the words uttered in the Upper Room refer: 'This is my body given up for you.... This is the cup of my blood shed for you....'"[58]

From this we can draw some understanding of what the doxology means.

Through Him: Only through Jesus' mediation do we have access to the Father (1 Tim 2:5). "No one can come to the Father except through Me" (John 14:6).

With Him: We are adopted sons and daughters in the Family of God. We are co-heirs with Christ (Romans 8:16-17) and without Him we can do nothing (John 15:5).

In Him: We must have Christ in us to have life in Him. Jesus says, "He who eats my Flesh and drinks my Blood lives in Me and I in him" (John 6:56).

---

58. John Paul II. *Mystery and Worship of the Eucharist*, 3.

Great Amen

All: AMEN!

Amen means "Yes, it's true!" or "I swear it is so!" **By saying "Amen," the community in effect says "Yes, I believe all that has been said."** In the Great Amen, we give assent to everything that has come before. As a group we affirm the real presence of the Eucharist which we will individually affirm later. In the fourth century in Rome, St. Jerome reported that the Great Amen was proclaimed with such force, it echoed like thunder and the pagan temples trembled! Let us exclaim our "Amen" with that power.

COMMUNION RITE

Lord's Prayer

Priest: Taught by our Savior's command and formed by the word of God, we dare to say:

All: Our Father, who art in heaven, hallowed be thy name; thy kingdom come; thy will be done on earth as it is in heaven. Give us this day our daily bread; and forgive us our trespasses as we forgive those who trespass against us; and lead us not into temptation, but deliver us from evil (Matthew 6:9-13; Luke 11).

Priest: Deliver us, Lord, from every evil, and grant us peace in our day. In your mercy keep us free from sin (John 17:15) and protect us from all anxiety as we wait in joyful hope for the coming of our Savior, Jesus Christ (Titus 2:13).

All: For the kingdom, the power, and the glory are yours, now and forever (Ephesians 3:21; Didache).

Most of us have spent at least a little time thinking about the Lord's Prayer, so I'll try not to bore you with the basics. Instead, let's consider three points many people don't realize about the Our Father as recited in the Mass.

The first item to consider is that calling God Father was a daring act when Jesus' was here on earth (John 5:18; 19:7). Even so, Christ not only called Him Father, but also taught us to do so (Matthew 6:9). Even today we should be honored, amazed indeed, to be able to call God our Father. He is the Supreme Being and mere mortals should not be able to speak about the Infinite Being, God, with such personal terms as father. Yet Jesus speaks of Him in the most intimate term, Abba (that is "Daddy"), and teaches us to do the same (Matthew 6:9-13; Luke 11:2-4). A seminary professor of mine, Fr. Aelred Kavanough, introduced the Lord's Prayer wonderfully at each Mass when he said, "Taught by our Savior's command and formed by the word of God, we DARE to say, Our Father…." This nicely sums up why we call God our Father and how privileged we are as sons and daughters to be able to call Him our Father.

The second area of interest is the phrase "give us this day our daily bread." Bread was the staple food in the area where Jesus lived, so going without bread usually meant having an empty stomach. Beyond this how-ever, the phrase refers not only to everyday physical nourishment but also to our spiritual food, the Eucharist. Jesus, in the Eucharist, is our Bread of life (John 6:35). In the same way that we need physical food to survive, our souls will suffer spiritual starvation if we don't receive Jesus in the Eucharist.

Third and finally, let's look at an item in the embolism prayer. The embolism prayer is the one that begins with "Deliver us, Lord from every evil…" This prayer reminds us that we can't do it all on our own. Only with God's help can you remain holy and pure. So deliver me from evil, Lord! The embolism prayer contains another interesting phrase, "we wait in joyful hope for the coming of our Savior, Jesus Christ." Do we honestly "wait in joyful hope" for the coming of Jesus? Many of us wait in hope for his coming in the Eucharist but how many of us wait in joyful hope for his second (eschatological) coming at the end of the world? Most people are scared of the end times. I never hear fellow students or my co-workers walking around saying, "I sure hope the world ends and Jesus comes again today!" If we are living a holy life, though, we have nothing to fear! It will be a time of great joy. So let us wait in joyful hope for our Savior's coming!

As we pray the Our Father, it is also important to remember the priests, our spiritual fathers here on earth. Our priests bring us new life in Baptism, feed us with the Bread of Life, and give us away in marriage. Clearly their role is much like that of our earthly fathers. Pray for them daily!

Sign of Peace

Priest: Lord Jesus Christ, you said to your apostles: I leave you peace, my peace I give you (John 14:27). Look not on our sins, but on the faith of your Church, and grant us the peace and unity of your kingdom where you live for ever and ever. All: Amen.

Priest: The peace of the Lord be with you always (John 20:19-20).
All: And also with you.
Deacon/Priest: Let us offer each other the sign of peace.

We follow the custom of saying "peace be with you" while shaking hands with those near us. This phrase, "peace be with you" was the Jewish way of saying "hello." Although our sign of peace to others in Mass generally consists of shaking their hands, this is not the only practice in the world. In some regions people bow their heads to each other, hug each other, or kiss. Yes, in some countries they really kiss.

The whole congregation is at the same level during the Sign of Peace. Physicians shake hands with homeless people. The Sabbath has always been the day of equality. Even in the time before Christianity, the ancient Jews saw slaves as being equal to their masters on the Sabbath day. No one was burdened by hard labor. It was a day of equality and freedom. Let us treat all members of Christ's Body with dignity and respect (1 Corinthians 12:12ff).

The Sign of Peace also brings unity and reconciliation (Matthew 5:24) to people of the community. This part of the Mass reminds us that we cannot be at peace with God unless we are at peace with one another. This common union with others should bring us into greater love for the Lord.

Fraction Rite

All: Lamb of God (John 1:36), you take away the sins of the world: have mercy on us (Matthew 20:30; Luke 17:13). Lamb of God (Is 53:7), you take away the sins of the world: have mercy on us (Matthew 15:22, Matthew 17:15). Lamb of God (Rev 5:6,12), you take away the sins of the world: grant us peace.

Also called the Lamb of God (Agnus Dei in Latin) or breaking of the bread, the **Fraction Rite symbolizes God becoming accessible to us.** When Jesus died the Temple veil in the Holy of Holies separating the people from God's presence was ripped from top to bottom (Luke 23:45). So Jesus, through fraction of his Body on the cross, tore down the division between us (the people) and Heaven (Holy of Holies). The breaking of the Host in Mass is analogous to Christ being broken on the cross and also of the Temple veil being ripped. Therefore through this fraction rite we are able to stand in God's presence and be part of his Family.

Since all the participants share in the one Bread of life, the congregation is bonded together. For in "sharing in one bread of life which is Christ, who died and rose for the salvation of the world, the many faithful are made one body (see 1 Corinthians 10:17)"[59] and "Through the breaking of the bread and the Communion of the faithful the unity of the faithful is expressed."[60]

While the Host is being broken, the priest places a small piece in the chalice containing Christ's Blood. This is called the Commingling. As he does this he says, "May this mingling of the Body and Blood of our Lord Jesus Christ bring eternal life to us who receive it." In the early Church, the pope or local bishop often sent pieces of the Eucharist from his Mass to his area churches to express the connection between all Masses worldwide. Also, a piece of Host from one Mass at a church was placed in the chalice of the next Mass at that church to show all Masses there are part of the one eternal sacrifice of Christ.

---

59. *General Instruction of the Roman Missal (2000)*, no. 83.
60. Ibid. no. 72.

This connection between Masses is displayed today as the priest gets more Hosts from the tabernacle. This happens when the priest does not consecrate enough altar bread at the Mass and must use the excess Hosts stored in the tabernacle from previous Masses. We store the Blessed Sacrament (Eucharist) in a tabernacle in order to protect it, for

> "The Catholic Church has always devoutly guarded as a most precious treasure the mystery of faith, that is, the ineffable gift of the Eucharist which she received from Christ her Spouse as a pledge of His immense love."[61]

Regarding the location of this tabernacle, the Instruction on the Worship of the Eucharist states that,

> "The place in a church...where the Blessed Sacrament is reserved in the tabernacle should be truly prominent. It ought to be suitable for private prayer so that the faithful may easily and fruitfully, by private devotion also, continue to honor our Lord in this sacrament."[62]

The Tabernacle mentioned in the Old Testament is not the same as our present day tabernacles. In the Old Testament times, the Tabernacle was a movable sanctuary or tent (before the Temple was built) of meeting (Ex 25-31, 35-40) that housed the Ark of the Covenant. Inside the tabernacle was the showbread, the altar of incense, the golden candlestick and the Ark behind the veil of Holy of Holies. Our modern day tabernacles are more like the Ark of the Covenant than the Old Testament Tabernacle. The Ark was a highly decorated sacred container that held the Israelites' most sacred possessions. The Ark's contents prefigured Christ while our tabernacles actually contain Him. Look at the following comparison:

---

61. Paul VI. *Mystery of Faith*. St. Paul, p. 5.
62. *Instruction on the Worship of the Eucharist*, 53.

Ark of the Covenant Contained:	*Our Tabernacles Contain:*
pieces of the tablets on which the Ten Commandments were written. The Ten Commandments were the center of the old law.	Jesus, the new and ultimate lawgiver that extended the Ten Commandments (Matthew 5).
Manna (bread) that dropped from Heaven. A cup similar to a ciborium was filled with manna and placed in the Ark of Covenant (Ex 16:33).	Jesus, the true bread from Heaven (John 6:32-35) is placed in a gold ciborium in the tabernacle.
Aaron's staff or rod that blossomed. This was a signal from God that He wanted Aaron to be priest.	Jesus Christ, who is the one true high priest (Hebrews 4:14).

Mary, the New Ark and Living Tabernacle

Just as the Ark of the Covenant contained items that prefigured Jesus, and our tabernacle now contains Jesus in the Eucharist, so Mary held Jesus in her womb for nine months. St. Luke goes to great lengths in his Gospel to show Mary is the fulfillment of the Ark of the Covenant. The following comparison should help:

Ark of the Covenant	*Mary, the New Ark*
"David says, 'How can the Ark of the Lord come to me?'" 2 Samuel 6:9.	"Elizabeth, filled with the Holy Spirit says, "How does this happen to me, that the mother of my Lord should come to me?'" Luke 1:43.
"The Ark of the Lord remained in the house of Obededom the Gittite for three months" 2 Samuel 6:11.	"Mary remained with her about three months and then returned to her home" Luke 1:56.
David leaps and dances before the Lord in the Ark. 2 Samuel 6:16	From Elizabeth's womb, John the Baptist leaps and dances before the Lord in Mary's womb. Luke 1:44

So is clear that Mary, because she held Jesus in her womb, is the new Ark of the Covenant. Not only is Mary the new Ark, she is also the new Eve. For in the same way that Eve convinced Adam to eat of the forbidden fruit which brought death upon us, so the new Eve, Mary, prompts us to eat the fruit, Jesus, of the tree of life, the cross (Revelation 2:7,9; Revelation Chp. 22). In fact the word "lady" is derived from the Anglo-Saxon "laef-da" which means "loaf-giver" or "bread-giver." Thus our Lady, Mary, gives us the Bread of Life, Jesus (John 6:51).[63]

Communion

Priest: This is the Lamb of God (Rev 5:6). This is Jesus who takes away the sins of the world. Happy are we who are called to his supper (Rev 19:9).

All: Lord, I am not worthy to receive you, but only say the word and I shall be healed (Matthew 8:8; Luke 7:7).

What is this supper that the priest mentions? Is it the Mass? Yes, it is the "wedding supper of the Lamb" (Rev. 19:9). As explained earlier, Heaven and earth are linked at this wedding supper, the Mass, where Jesus the Lamb of God is united to his Bride the Church. Now look and see how this wedding of the Lamb to the Church plays out in Mass:

Mass	*Wedding of Lamb*
Penitential Rite is the part of Mass where the congregation is cleansed of venial sins.	Because the congregation, that is the Church, is being forgiven of sins, the Bride of Christ is being purified. Christ deserves the best, so only a perfect, pure Bride will be acceptable to Jesus.

---

63. A couple of items in the preceding paragraph come from Kaczmarek's *Hidden Treasure*, p.88.

Gloria is the part of Mass in which we thank the Lord for making us sinless.

The Bride thanks Christ for making her beautiful and pure.

First Reading is the section of Mass in which God is revealed to us in a limited way. Through this reading, we begin to understand who God is.

God gives his Bride a glimpse of who he really is. He moves a little closer to her.

Responsorial Psalm allows us to respond in song to God's revelation to us.

The Bride thanks God for letting her meet Him and responds with a love song.

Second Reading is where Jesus moves into our lives. We grow deeper in our understanding and love for Christ.

As Groom, Jesus gets closer to his Bride, she is filled with joyous love. They are now building a relationship together.

Gospel is the pinnacle of God's revelation to us.
Here is where Jesus' life is fully opened up before our eyes.

Jesus, the Groom, pledges his love for us. In return, He asks us, his Bride, to love Him. This is the request of engagement; He wants us to devote ourselves to Him in marriage.

Profession of Faith is our commitment to all God has shown us. The creed contains the basic assertions of the faith.

Here the Bride accepts the request of engagement by pledging herself totally to Christ, the Groom. The word "creed" literally means "I give my heart," so we the Bride pledge our heart to Christ as we recite the Creed.

Preparation of Gifts is the place in the Mass where we give all of our gifts to God.

Not only does the Bride pledge her love, she also gives all her gifts, even the gift of her own life, to Christ. In the process of drawing closer to Him, we, the Bride, become more like Him.

Consecration is the part in which Jesus' love is so great, He must be joined with us. Consequently, He becomes truly present under the appearance of bread.

Jesus, the Groom, proclaims that his life will be given up for us, his Bride.

Communion is the long awaited event of the Holy Mass. At Communion, Christ comes to us personally under the appearance of bread. Then we receive and consume (eat) the Body of Christ, becoming one spirit in Christ (1 Corinthians 6:17).

This is the event the Bride and Groom have been waiting for: the honeymoon. Christ the Groom offers his whole being to his Bride saying, "This is my Body." By consuming (eating) the wedding feast of Christ's Body, we the Bride bring about the consummation of the marriage. Just as a bride and groom "are no longer two, but one flesh" (Matthew 19:6; Genesis 2:24) in their marriage, Jesus becomes "one spirit" with his Bride, the Church, in the Wedding Supper of the Lamb.

Thus we can see some general movements in the Mass. In the Liturgy of Word (especially in the readings), God personally speaks to us. We respond to his call in the Profession of Faith. In the Liturgy of the Eucharist, we offer ourselves to Him at the procession of the gifts and He offers Himself to us at Communion. Thus the Liturgy of the Word is equivalent to the courtship or dating process while the Liturgy of the Eucharist pertains to the marriage between the Lamb and his Church.

Have you ever noticed what girls wear to their first Communion? They wear white dresses and veils. Where else will they wear attire such as this? At their weddings. The first Communion is the first union with Christ in the Eucharist. As we have seen, this is like a marriage. So the girls wear wedding garments to their first Communion.

Now let's get back to the words of the Mass. The phrase "Lord I am not worthy to receive you" brings a whole mix of emotions to the heart. Love for the Eucharist pulls us toward that Blessed Sacrament while our sins push us away from it. We are aware of our unworthiness, but nevertheless we pray the Lord will "say the word" so we can receive Him.

We respond with, "Lord, I am not worthy to receive you, but only say the word and I shall be healed." But what is this word? Actually it is not one word but a group of words. The Mass text in question comes from the healing of the centurion's servant found in Matthew chapter 8 and Luke chapter 7. These passages tell of a centurion (one in charge of 100 soldiers) whose faithful servant was near death. In asking Jesus to heal his servant, the centurion showed great humility and faith. The centurion tells Jesus, "Lord, I am not worthy to have you enter under my roof; only say the word and my servant will be healed." After a remark about the centurion's great faith, Jesus issues the long awaited words, "You may go; as you have believed, let it be done for you" (Matthew 8:13). Like the centurion who said he was unworthy for Jesus to come into his home, we recognize and assert our unworthiness to receive Christ in the Eucharist. But if we have humility, purity, and faith, Jesus will invite us to receive his Body and Blood with the same words He issued to the centurion, "You may go; as you have believed, let it be done for you." Then we may partake of his eternal gift.

The communion song (or antiphon) begins as the priest receives the Eucharist under both species and then comes forward to distribute

Communion. In exceptional circumstances, commissioned lay people known as extraordinary ministers may help the priest to distribute the Body and Blood. Circumstances that may cause such a need include the lack of an ordinary minister (bishop, priest, or deacon), the inability of ordinary ministers to distribute Communion because of sickness or old age, or not having enough ordinary ministers to serve an extremely large number of people desiring to receive Holy Communion.[64]

As we come forward to receive Communion, several similarities between our actions here and other parts of the Mass should come to mind. In the presentation of the gifts, our self-offering was brought forward to the altar. Here at Communion we again bring that offering as we walk toward the altar. As we offer our lives to Christ, He offers Himself back to us. Earlier in Mass the Host was elevated, proclaimed to be Jesus' Body and Blood, and the congregation responds with the Great Amen. At Communion, these actions and words are repeated but on a personal level. The minister elevates the Host and says "the Body of Christ." The Communicant (the person receiving Communion) affirms this statement with a personal "Amen." The "Amen" that the communicant pronounces upon receiving the sacred Host is the equivalent of saying "Yes, I believe."

Those coming forward to receive the Eucharist should bow or make another appropriate sign of reverence before receiving the Host. This sign of reverence not only shows recognition of Christ's presence under the form of bread, but also gives Him due respect. Communicants, that is those receiving Communion, may receive the Host in their hands or on their tongues. Whichever way one chooses, the key is to be respectful. If one receives in the hands, follow St. Cyril's advice to make your hands into a throne to receive Jesus, our King. If the faithful are to receive the sacred Blood also, the communicant comes to the minister who holds the chalice up and says, "The Blood of Christ." The communicant responds with "Amen," professing faith in the sacrament. Through Communion, the

64. *General Instruction of the Roman Missal (2000)*, no. 162.

faithful receive the Lord's body and blood in the same way that the apostles received Communion from Christ's own hands.

You have just received the Body and Blood of Christ. What a miracle! Jesus Christ, the God-Man, has given Himself to you. How much closer to our Lord can we be while still on earth? This food is unlike any other food. Normally when we eat food it becomes part of us, but when we eat the Body of Christ, we become part of it! By receiving the Body of Christ (Eucharist) we are brought into the mystical body of Christ (Church). Sharing of his Body and Blood signifies union with Him, for He wants us to share in his Flesh and Blood, to become his brothers and sisters. Or as the Catechism puts it, "Communion with the Holy Trinity and fraternal communion are inseparably the fruit of the Spirit in the liturgy."[65]

Purification

After Communion, the priest returns to the altar and collects any remaining particles of the Eucharist (John 6:12). He purifies

> "the paten or vessel over the chalice, then cleanses the chalice…It is also permitted, especially if there are several vessels to be cleansed, to leave them suitably covered on a corporal, either at the altar or at a side table and to cleanse them immediately after Mass following the dismissal of the people."[66]

In silence the priest prays:
Lord, may I receive these gifts in purity of heart. May they bring me healing and strength, now and for ever.

Silence may be appropriate at this time. Silence is one of the most neglected treasures of our time. Some people find beauty and depth in

---

65. *Catechism of the Catholic Church*, par. 1108.
66. *General Instruction of the Roman Missal (2000)*, no. 163.

silence while others are uncomfortable even during a brief pause. These uncomfortable people sniffle or cough just to hear noise. So what can we do during this quiet time? How can one benefit from it? These quiet times can be outstanding opportunities to reach into the depths of your soul and examine yourself. Here we can grow closer to Jesus, for since we have just received Him the Eucharist He is with us in the highest sense. Our silent prayers are often the purest of our prayers. Find a quiet spot and spend a few minutes in silence.

Prayer After Communion

Priest: Let us pray. Lord Jesus Christ, you give us your Body and Blood in the Eucharist as a sign that even now we share your life. May we come to possess it completely in the kingdom where you live for ever and ever. All: Amen.

Every Sunday I see people headed out to the parking lot immediately after Communion. These are often the same people who are still at the stadium watching the third overtime period of the Broncos and Cowboys game during a rainstorm. There is even a nickname that has arisen for this early exit, the Judas shuffle. This name came about because just like Judas (in John 13:30), these people eat and run. They don't wait for the end of the meal. Please don't leave early!

A saintly priest once saw a man leaving Mass after Communion and sent the altar servers to escort him with candles. The priest's point was to show that since the man had just received Communion, Jesus was still present in him. ☺ Such embarrassment could be headed your way if you choose to leave too early.

As we reach the conclusion of the Mass, it is a good time to reflect back on what has happened. In the Mass, we see at least a shadow of each of the seven Sacraments.

Mass and the Seven Sacraments

1. *Baptism*—While entering the church each of us dipped a hand in holy water and made the sign of the cross. This act recalls our Baptism, where the two key elements are holy water and the words 'I Baptize you in the name of the Father, and of the Son, and of the Holy Spirit' (Matthew 28:19).

2. *Confirmation*—Just before the consecration, in the section of Mass called the epiclesis, the ordained minister (priest) prays over the bread and wine, requesting that the Lord's "Spirit come upon these gifts to make them holy." Later we receive this holy gift of the Holy Spirit in the form of the Eucharist. In Confirmation, the ordained minister of Christ (bishop) prays over the person being confirmed and requests that they "be sealed with the gift of the Holy Spirit." That person then receives the gift(s) of the Holy Spirit.

3. *Reconciliation*—This sacrament is also known as Penance or Confession. It flows from the need to be pure so that one can receive Christ in Mass and for our souls to be pure for Heaven. Earlier in Mass, we saw that the Penitential (which comes from the word Penance) Rite is a mini-confession. It forgives us from venial sins. Pope John Paul II writes,

   "It is not only that Penance leads to the Eucharist, but that the Eucharist also leads to Penance. For when we realize who it is that we receive in Eucharistic Communion, there springs up in us almost spontaneously a sense of unworthiness, together with sorrow for our sins and an interior need for purification."[67]

4. *Eucharist*—The Mass and the Eucharist are so intertwined that the Mass is often called the Eucharist. The Eucharist is most often received at Mass.

---

67. John Paul II. *Mystery and Worship of the Eucharist*, 7.

5. *Marriage*—The Mass is the Wedding Supper of the Lamb. In our celebration Christ the Lamb of God marries his Bride the Church.

6. *Holy Orders*—The Mass is led by a priest or bishop, both are men of Holy Orders. The faithful lay people most frequently come into contact with a man in Holy Orders when at Mass.

7. *Anointing of the Sick*—St. Ignatius of Antioch in 110 A.D. called the Eucharist the "medicine of immortality." Further, the basic format of the rite of Anointing follows the same outline as the Mass. Finally, many times in this Sacrament of the sick, the Eucharist that was formed in our Mass is received by the sick who could not attend.

As you may have noticed, "All other liturgical rites and all the works of the Christian life are linked with the eucharistic celebration, flow from it, and have it as their end."[68] The Mass sanctifies us, builds the Mystical Body of Christ, and gives worship to God. The Sacraments draw power from the paschal mystery as Christ's grace flows from his Passion, Death, Resurrection and Ascension. The Instruction on the Worship of the Eucharist states it this way:

"the celebration of the Eucharist is the true center of the whole Christian life both for the universal Church and for the local congregation of that Church. For 'the other sacraments, as indeed every ministry of the Church and every work of the apostolate, are linked with the Eucharist and are directed towards it. For the Eucharist contains the entire spiritual good of the Church, namely, Christ himself, our Passover and living bread, offering his flesh, living and life-giving in the Spirit, life to men who are thus invited and led on to offer themselves, their labors and all created things together with him.'"[69]

---

68. *General Instruction of the Roman Missal (2000)*, par. 16.
69. *Instruction on the Worship of the Eucharist, 6.*

CONCLUDING RITES

Greeting

Priest: The Lord be with you.
All: And also with you.

Those of you who are Star Trek or Star Wars fans know how to give such stylish greetings as "Live long and prosper," and "May the Force be with you." But the greeting we receive here at the tail end of Mass is far superior. What could be a better greeting than wishing that the Lord be with that person?

Even after all of my attempts to make the Mass interesting and beneficial to you, I realize there will still be some who will ask the question, "Why do we have to go to Mass?" I have so far tried to show why one should want to go the holy Sacrifice, without emphasizing that Catholics are obligated to attend Mass on Sunday. The "Sunday obligation" rule is meant to be a reminder for those who tend to carelessly forget to give God at least a minimum amount of public attention. Mass on Sunday usually takes only one hour out of the 168 available in a week. Surely this isn't too much to ask, is it? But since there will always be some who want to know why we have to go, I'll do my best to give a series of reasons why regular Mass attendance is beneficial and necessary.

How long could you survive without food? Most people could survive about a week without physical nourishment. In a similar way, the Lord knows the majority of people can survive at most about a week without spiritual nourishment. We need the grace of the Eucharist so we don't spiritually starve. Our sins take the grace from our souls. The Sacraments, especially Eucharist and Penance, are where our souls are "reloaded" with Christ's grace. So weekly Mass attendance and participation is the minimum that will keep most people "spiritually alive."[70]

The Ten Commandments make up the basic guide to our moral lives. The third commandment says, "Remember to keep holy the Sabbath day" (Exodus 20:8). We dedicate every Sunday, the new Sabbath (as the day of the Resurrection), to the Lord. Following the ancient interpretation of this command, all Jews and Christians give public attention to God on their Sabbath (including Jesus–see Luke 4:16). Our Mass is not just attention given to God, it is true worship of Him. The first step for Catholics in keeping holy the Lord's Day is participating in Mass. This commandment excludes someone from saying, "I just forgot to go to Mass" since the command itself is to remember!

One may say, "Yeah, but can't I just pray by myself at home?" St. Paul would have had a heart attack if he heard someone trying to justify such a position! You can and should pray at home everyday, but that is no substitute for Mass. The position that says 'if I have faith within myself, I don't need to participate in an organized church,' is **not** a theologically or biblically sustainable position. Personal faith is essential, but it is never exclusively individual. When Jesus healed the sick and crippled, it was often the faith of the sick person's friends and family that brought about the healing. For instance, Jesus saw the faith of the people who brought in the paralytic and through this healed him and forgave his sins (Matthew 9:1-7).

Look also at our practice of infant Baptism. The faith of the parents and godparents sustains the child for years before the child is ever capable of having personal faith. All of God's revelation is rooted in family and community. Certainly we must participate in the community of faith, the

---

70. Catholic are obliged to receive the Eucharist only once a year, but weekly or even daily reception has always been advised.

Church that Christ established (see Matthew 16:18; 18:17-18; 1 Tim 3:15)! As a Catholic community, the one activity we all attend and participate in is Sunday Mass. All Catholics must join us!

Most scholars agree that the passage which reads "We should not stay away from our assembly" (Hebrews 10:25) refers to the Eucharistic assembly or as we call it now, Mass. Further, in the sixth chapter of John's Gospel Christ plainly says, "I am the living bread that came down from heaven; whoever eats this bread will live forever; and the bread that I will give is my flesh for the life of the world." Then he says, "Amen, amen, I say to you, unless you eat the flesh of the Son of Man and drink his blood, you do not have life within you. Whoever eats my flesh and drinks my blood has eternal life, and I will raise him up on the last day. For my flesh is true food, and my blood is true drink. Whoever eats my flesh and drinks my blood remains in me and I in him" (John 6:51,53-56). The only normal way to follow this command Jesus issued is to go to Mass.

At the Last Supper Christ tells us, "Do this in remembrance of me." St. Paul explains, "For as often as you eat this bread and drink the cup, you proclaim the death of the Lord until he comes" (1 Corinthians 11:25-26). What do we have to do in remembrance? The Last Supper. It is re-presented (along with the paschal mystery) at the Mass. We must celebrate this event as Jesus commanded.

So the obligation to attend the Eucharistic celebration (which is another name for Mass) can obviously be seen in Scripture and in the life of the early Church from which the Bible came. What Scripture does not tell us is exactly how often we must go. We know that we must go at some time (Luke 22:19; John 6:51-58) and that going often is good (1 Corinthians 11:25-26 connected to 1 Corinthians 2:2), but what is the minimum amount that we must go?

Many in the early Church believed weekly Sunday attendance should be the rule. The first day of the week, Sunday, has prominence because of the Resurrection (Matthew 28:1; Acts 20:7; Rev 1:10 and numerous reputable early Christian writings). Others, however, held that daily attendance was needed in imitation of the Apostles and the early converts to Christianity (Acts 2:46).

The Church eventually decided that weekly attendance was necessary but one is still free to go daily. Therefore the necessity of Mass attendance is grounded in Scripture (and grounded in the life of the early Church), while the frequency of such attendance was to some degree worked out in the life and by the authority of the Church (Matthew 16:13-19; 18:15-20).

Blessing

Priest: May almighty God bless you, the Father, and the Son, and the Holy Spirit (Matthew 28:19).
All: Amen (1 Chronicles 16:36).

As we continue to reflect back over the Mass, it becomes clearer why the Mass is the supreme action of the Church. We see that it is the primary act of response to the love God the Father issues. In the mystery of the Trinity, God the Father gives perfect life and love and in doing so eternally begets the Son, the Eternal Word. This is a giving of Himself, the Father, for He is perfect life and love. The Son, as the Second person of the Trinity and the perfect image of the Father does the same thing as the Father; He returns perfect life and love to the Father.

The Mass is an essential part of this divine action, for in it Christ, the Son, true God and true man, offers Himself to God the Father for the sake of his Bride, the Church. Jesus was sacrificed at the Crucifixion and that sacrifice is eternal. He stands as the slain Lamb in Heaven (Rev 5:6) forever and ever. This sacrifice took place so that our sins, the sins of Christ's Bride the Church, would be forgiven. Instead of us suffering, Christ put our burden on his holy shoulders and offered Himself to God the Father. "No greater love can a man have than to give his life for a friend" (John 15:13). Now Christ's Bride is pure because of what He did and his spotless Bride is worthy to be his wife.

The offering that Christ makes of his own life to the Father is also eternal. It is the same action He makes as He returns the perfect life and love to the Father, for He is this perfect life and love. Jesus gives Himself in the Trinity just as God the Father gave Himself to the Son. This not only takes place in Heaven, it also takes place on the altar at Mass. Christ is offered to the Father by his earthly servant, the priest, who stands in his place (in persona Christi). Therefore, because the Mass imitates the perfect action, the action that takes place within the Most Holy Trinity, it is the highest action that we as humans can participate in here on earth.

Dismissal

Deacon/Priest: The Mass is ended, go in peace (Luke 7:50; 2 Kings 5:19) to love and serve the Lord (2 Chronicles 35:3; Matthew 5:34).
All: Thanks be to God (2 Corinthians 9:15).

Some people assert that the word "Mass" comes from the Hebrew term "missach" which means "free offering." Most scholars, however, believe the word "Mass" comes from the Latin phrase "Ite missa est" which means either "Go, this is the dismissal" or "Go, it is sent." This phrase comes from the last line of the Liturgy in which the people are commissioned and sent out to love and serve the Lord. First used in the fourth century, the word "Mass" points to our mission from God (like the Blues Brothers) and is a term used mostly in our Latin Rite. Other parts of the Church call the Mass the breaking of the bread, the Eucharist, the Lord's Supper, the Agape, the Sacrifice, or the (Divine) Liturgy.

The congregation shouldn't go out into the parking lot and cut each other off trying to exit the fastest. The Mass should transform us into better people in our daily lives, not just in the church building. Don't be good only on Sundays. That's hypocritical. It's schizophrenic. The Mass calls us to love and serve the Lord by loving and serving one another (Matthew 25) in everyday life.

Pope John Paul II puts it this way,

> "[E]ucharistic worship constitutes the soul of all Christian life. In fact, Christian life is expressed in the fulfilling of the greatest commandment, that is to say, in the love of God and neighbor, and this love finds its source in the Blessed Sacrament, which is commonly called the sacrament of love. The Eucharist signifies this charity, and therefore recalls it, makes it present and at the same time brings it about"[71]

Recession

As the music plays, the priest standing in persona Christi kisses the altar (standing for God the Father). After Christ (represented by the priest) shows his love for the Father (represented by the altar) and draws strength from Him, He leads the way out into the world. The Mass has changed our lives. Now we are on a mission to transform the world. We the people of God follow the priest out to win souls for Jesus Christ.

---

71. John Paul II. *Mystery and Worship of the Eucharist*, 5.

CONCLUSION

The question will inevitably arise, "What is the Mass?" Although this question seems nearly impossible to answer in any concise fashion, the Instruction on the Worship of the Eucharist gives an admirable answer with the following explanation:

> "Our Saviour at the Last Supper on the night when he was betrayed instituted the eucharistic sacrifice of his Body and Blood so that he might perpetuate the sacrifice of the cross throughout the centuries till his coming. He thus entrusted to the Church, his beloved spouse, a memorial of his death and resurrection: a sacrament of love, a sign of unity, a bond of charity, a paschal meal in which Christ is eaten, the mind filled with grace and a pledge of future glory given to us.'
>
> Hence the Mass, the Lord's Supper, is at the same time and inseparably: a sacrifice in which the sacrifice of the cross is perpetuated; a memorial of the death and resurrection of the Lord, who said 'do this in memory of me' (Luke. 22:19); a sacred banquet in which, through the communion of the Body and Blood of the Lord, the People of God share the benefits of the Paschal Sacrifice, renew the New Covenant which God has made with man once for all through the Blood of Christ, and in faith and hope foreshadow and anticipate the eschatological banquet in the kingdom of the Father, proclaiming the Lord's death 'till his coming.'"[72]

---

72. *Instruction on the Worship of the Eucharist, 3a and Constitution on the Sacred Liturgy*, art. 47.

Other questions will also arise, such as "Why did you write this book, Dave?" and "Why should I read it?" "Why should I study the Mass?" or "Why do I need to go to Mass?" The answer to all of these and many more questions can be found in the following simple ideas: Understanding the Mass leads to love for the Mass. Love for the Mass leads to love of Christ. Love of Christ leads to Heaven.

Appendix: Other Eucharistic Prayers

Eucharistic Prayer I

We come to you Father, with praise and thanksgiving, through Jesus Christ your Son. Through him we ask you to accept and bless these gifts we offer you in sacrifice. We offer them for your holy catholic Church, watch over it, Lord, and guide it; grant it peace and unity throughout the world. We offer them for John Paul our Pope, for N. our bishop, and for all who hold and teach the catholic faith that comes to us from the apostles. Remember, Lord, your people, especially those for whom we now pray, N. and N. Remember all of us gathered here before you. You know how firmly we believe in you and dedicate ourselves to you. We offer you this sacrifice of praise for ourselves and those who are dear to us. We pray to you, our living and true God, for our well-being and redemption. In union with the whole Church we honor Mary, the ever-virgin mother of Jesus Christ our Lord and God. We honor Joseph, her husband, the apostles and martyrs Peter and Paul, Andrew and all the saints. May their merits and prayers gain us your constant help and protection. Father, accept this offering from your whole family. Grant us your peace in this life, save us from final damnation, and count us among those you have chosen. Bless and approve our offering; make it acceptable to you, an offering in spirit and in truth. Let it become for us the body and blood of Jesus Christ, your only Son, our Lord. The day before he suffered he took bread in his sacred hands and looking up to heaven, to you, his almighty Father, he gave you thanks and praise. He broke the bread, gave it to his disciples, and said: Take this, all of you, and eat it: this is my body which will be given up for you. When supper was ended, he took the cup. Again he gave you thanks and praise, gave the cup to his disciples, and said: Take this, all of you, and drink from it: this is the cup of my blood, the blood of the new and everlasting covenant. It will be shed for you and for all so that sins may be forgiven. Do this in memory of me. Let us proclaim the mystery of faith.

[one of four Memorial Acclamations is proclaimed]

Father, we celebrate the memory of Christ, your Son. We, your people and your ministers, recall his passion, his resurrection from the dead, and his ascension into glory; and from the many gifts you have given us we offer to you, God of glory and majesty, this holy and perfect sacrifice: the bread of life and the cup of eternal salvation. Look with favor on these offerings and accept them as once you accepted the gifts of your servant Abel, the sacrifice of Abraham, our father in faith, and the bread and wine offered by your priest Melchisedech. Almighty God, we pray that your angel may take this sacrifice to your altar in heaven. Then, as we receive from this altar the sacred body and blood of your Son, let us be filled with every grace and blessing. Remember, Lord, those who have died and have gone before us marked with the sign of faith, especially those for whom we now pray, N. and N. May these and all who sleep in Christ, find in your presence light, happiness, and peace. For ourselves, too, we ask some share in the fellowship of your apostles and martyrs, with John the Baptist, Stephen, Matthias, Barnabas, and all the saints. Though we are sinners, we trust in your mercy and love. Do not consider what we truly deserve, but grant us your forgiveness. Through Christ our Lord. Through him you give us all these gifts. You fill them with life and goodness, you bless them and make them holy.

Eucharistic Prayer III

Father, you are holy indeed, and all creation rightly gives you praise. All life, all holiness comes from you through your Son, Jesus Christ our Lord, by the working of the Holy Spirit. From age to age you gather a people to yourself so that from east to west a perfect offering may be made to the glory of your name. And so, Father, we bring you these gifts. We ask you to make them holy by the power of your Spirit, that they may become the body and blood of your Son, your Lord Jesus Christ, at whose command we celebrate this Eucharist. On the night he was betrayed, he took bread and gave you thanks and praise. He broke the bread, gave it to his disciples, and said: Take this, all of you, and eat it: this is my body which will be given up for you. When supper was ended, he took the cup. Again he gave you thanks and praise, gave the cup to his disciples, and said: Take this, all of you, and drink from it: this is the cup of my blood, the blood of the new and everlasting covenant. It will be shed for you and for all so that sins may be forgiven. Do this in memory of me. Let us proclaim the mystery of faith.

[one of four Memorial Acclamations is proclaimed]

Father, calling to mind the death your Son endured for our salvation, his glorious resurrection and ascension into heaven, and ready to greet him when he comes again, we offer you in thanksgiving this holy and living sacrifice. Look with favor on your Church's offering, and see the Victim whose death has reconciled us to yourself. Grant that we, who are nourished by his body and blood, may be filled with his Holy Spirit, and become one body, one spirit in Christ. May he make us an everlasting gift to you and enable us to share in the inheritance of your saints, with Mary, the virgin mother of God; with the apostles, the martyrs, and all your saints, on whose constant intercession we rely for help. Lord, may this sacrifice, which has made our peace with you, advance the peace and salvation of all the world. Strengthen in faith and love your pilgrim Church on earth; your servant, Pope John Paul, our bishop N., and all the bishops, with the clergy and the entire people your Son has gained for you. Father, hear the prayers of the family you have gathered here before you. In mercy and love unite all your children wherever they may be. Welcome into your kingdom our departed brothers and sisters, and all who have left this world in your friendship. We hope to enjoy for ever the vision of your glory, through Christ our Lord, from whom all good things come.

Eucharistic Prayer IV

Father, we acknowledge your greatness: all your actions show your wisdom and love. You formed man in your own likeness and set him over the whole world to serve you, his creator, and to rule over all creatures. Even when he disobeyed you and lost your friendship you did not abandon him to the power of death, but helped all men to seek and find you. Again and again you offered a covenant to man, and through the prophets taught him to hope for salvation. Father, you so loved the world that in the fullness of time you sent your only Son to be our Savior. He was conceived through the power of the Holy Spirit, and born of the Virgin Mary, a man like us in all things but sin. To the poor he proclaimed the good news of salvation, to prisoners, freedom, and to those in sorrow, joy. In fulfillment of your will he gave himself up to death; but by rising from the dead, he destroyed death and restored life. And that we might live no longer for ourselves but for him, he sent the Holy Spirit from you, Father, as his first gift to those who believe, to complete his work on earth and bring us the fullness of grace. Father, may this Holy Spirit sanctify these offerings. Let them become the body and blood of Jesus Christ our Lord as we celebrate the great mystery which he left us as an everlasting covenant. He always loved those who were his own in the world. When the time came for him to be glorified by you, his heavenly Father, he showed the depth of his love. While they were at supper, he took bread, said the blessing, broke the bread, and gave it to his disciples, saying: Take this, all of you, and eat it:

this is my body which will be given up for you. In the same way, he took the cup, filled with wine. He gave you thanks, and giving the cup to his disciples, said: Take this, all of you, and drink from it: this is the cup of my blood, the blood of the new and everlasting covenant. It will be shed for you and for all so that sins may be forgiven. Do this I memory of me. Let us proclaim the mystery of faith:

[one of four Memorial Acclamations is proclaimed]

Father, we now celebrate this memorial of our redemption. We recall Christ's death, his descent among the dead, his resurrection, and his ascension to your right hand; and, looking forward to his coming in glory, we offer you his body and blood, the acceptable sacrifice which brings salvation to the whole world. Lord, look upon this sacrifice which you have given to your Church; and by your Holy Spirit, gather all who share this one bread and one cup into the one body of Christ, a living sacrifice of praise. Lord, remember those for whom we offer this sacrifice, especially John Paul our Pope, N. our bishop, and bishops and clergy everywhere. Remember those who take part in this offering, those here present and all your people, and all who seek you with a sincere heart. Remember those who have died in the peace of Christ and all the dead whose faith is known to you alone. Father, in your mercy grant also to us, your children, to enter into our heavenly inheritance in the company of the Virgin Mary, the Mother of God, and your apostles and saints. Then, in your kingdom, freed from the corruption of sin and death, we shall sing your glory with every creature through Christ our Lord through whom you give us everything that is good. Through him, with him, in him, in the unity of the Holy Spirit, all glory and honor is yours, almighty Father, for ever and ever.

Bibliography

Barbaric, Slavko, O.F.M., Fr. *Celebrate Mass With Your Heart*. Milford, OH: Faith, 1994.

Belmonte, Charles. *Understanding the Mass*. Princeton: Scepter, 1989.

Butler, Alban; Herbert Thurston, S.J.; and Donald Attwater. *Butler's Lives of the Saints Complete Edition*. New York: P.J. Kenedy & Sons, 1963.

Cantalamessa, Raniero. *The Eucharist: Our Sanctification*. Collegeville, MN: Liturgical, 1995.

Catechism of the Catholic Church. Liguori, MO: Liguori, 1994.

Clements, Ronald E. *Exodus* (commentary). London: Cambridge, 1972.

Cochem, Martin von, Fr. *The Incredible Catholic Mass*. Rockford IL: Tan, 1997.

Congregation for the Doctrine of the Faith. *Dominus Iesus: On the Unicity and Salvific Universality of Jesus Christ and the Church*. Available at: http://www.vatican.va/roman_curia/congregations/cfaith/documents/rc_con_cfaith_doc_20000806_dominus-iesus_en.html. August 6, 2000.

Danielou, Jean S.J. *The Bible and the Liturgy*. Notre Dame, IN: U. of Notre Dame, 1956.

Deiss, Lucien. *It's the Lord's Supper*. New York: Paulist, 1976.

Effing, Myron. "Christ's Peace Offering." *This Rock*. May/June 2000: 14-17.

Emminghaus, Johannes H. *The Eucharist: Essence, Form, Celebration*. Collegeville, MN: Liturgical, 1978.

Federation of Diocesan Liturgical Commissions in cooperation with the Bishops' Committee on the Liturgy. *The Mystery of Faith: A Study of the Structural Elements of the Order of the Mass*. 1981.

Fischer, Balthasar. *Signs, Words & Gestures*. New York: Pueblo, 1981.

Flannery, Austin, ed. *Vatican Council II: The Conciliar and Post Conciliar Documents*. New rev. ed. Vol 1. Collegeville, MN: Liturgical Press, 1992.

General Instruction of the Roman Missal (English translation). National Conference of Catholic Bishops, 2000.

Gibbons, James Cardinal. *The Faith of Our Fathers*. Rockford, IL: Tan, 1980.

Guardini, Romano. *Preparing Yourself for Mass*. Manchester, NH: Sophia, 1993.

Guernsey, Daniel P, compiler. *Adoration*. San Francisco: Ignatius, 1999.

Hahn, Scott. "A Day with Scott Hahn." St. Paul's Apologetics Group. St. Agnes Catholic Church. Baton Rouge, LA, 19 Feb. 2000.

—. *A Father Who Keeps His Promises*. Ann Arbor, MI: Servant, 1998.

—. *Heaven's Mass*. Audio Tapes. West Covina, CA: St. Joseph, 1999.

—. *How to Get More Out of Mass*. Audio Tapes. West Covina, CA: St. Joseph.

—. "The Hunt for the Fourth Cup." *This Rock* Sept. 1991: cover, 7-12.

—. *The Lamb's Supper: the Mass as Heaven on Earth*. New York: Doubleday, 1999.

—. "The Lamb's Supper: Understanding the Mass." Video tape. West Covina, CA: St. Joseph.

—. (1998). Meal of Melchezidek. EWTN Library [On-line]. Available: http://www.ewtn.com/library/scriptur/eucharist.TXT

Hahn, Scott and Tim Staples. *All Things Catholic—Volume 1*. Audio Tapes. St. Joseph, 1999

Hardon, John, S.J. *The Catholic Catechism*. New York: Doubleday, 1981.

—. *The Treasury of Catholic Wisdom*. San Francisco: Ignatius, 1995.

Holy Bible: Revised Standard Version, Catholic Edition. San Francisco: Ignatius, 1966.

John Paul II. *The Mystery and Worship of the Eucharist*. Boston: Pauline, 1980.

Johnson, Kevin O. Ph.D. *Expressions of the Catholic Faith*. New York: Ballantine, 1994.

Jurgens, William A. *The Faith of the Early Fathers (Volume 1)*. Collegeville, MN: Liturgical, 1970.

Kaczmarek, Louis. *Hidden Treasure*. Manassas, VA: Trinity, 1990.

Kane, John A. *Transforming Your Life Through the Eucharist*. Manchester, NH: Sophia, 1999.

Kelley, Bennet, C.P., Rev. *Saint Joseph Baltimore Catechism (Revised Edition No. 2)*. New York: Catholic, 1969.

Kilmartin, Edward J., S.J. *The Eucharist in the Primitive Church*. Englewood Cliffs, NJ: Prentice-Hall, 1965.

Kodell, Jerome, O.S.B. *The Eucharist in the New Testament*. Collegeville, MN: Liturgical, 1988.

Kolodziej, Maynard, O.F.M., Fr. *Understanding the Mass*. Pulaski, WN: Franciscan, 1987.

Lewis, C. S. *The Four Loves*. London: Geoffrey Bles Ltd., 1960.

Loret, Pierre, C.S.S.R. *How the Mass Came to Be: From the Last Supper to Today's Eucharist*. Liguouri, MO: Liguori, 1985.

—. *The Story of the Mass: From the Last Supper to the Present Day*. Liguouri, MO: Liguori, 1982.

Marcetteau, S. S. *The Young Seminarian*. Paterson, NJ: St. Anthony Guild, 1943.

McGloin, Joseph, S.J. *How to Get More Out of the Mass*. Chicago: Loyola, 1989.

Meagher, James Rev., D.D. *How Christ Said the First Mass*. South Bend, IN: Marian, 1978 and Rockford, IL: Tan, 1984.

New American Bible. New York: Catholic, 1992.

Nichols, Aidan, O.P. *The Holy Eucharist*. Dublin, Ireland: Veritas, 1991.

O'Conner, James T. *The Hidden Manna*. San Francisco: Ignatius, 1988.

Paul VI. *Mystery of Faith*. Boston: St. Paul, 1965.

Randolph, Fr. Francis. *Know Him in the Breaking of the Bread*. San Francisco: Ignatius, 1998.

Ratzinger, Joseph Cardinal. *The Spirit of the Liturgy*. San Francisco: Ignatius, 2000.

Romero, Mario Fr. *Unabridged Christianity*. Santa Barbara: Queenship, 1999.

Sheed, Frank J. *Theology for Beginners 3rd Ed*. Ann Arbor, MI: Servant, 1981.

Smolarski, Dennis, S.J. *How Not to Say Mass*. New York: Paulist, 1986.

Speyr, Adrienne von. *The Holy Mass*. San Francisco: Ignatius, 1999.

Stravinskas, Peter Rev. *The Bible and the Mass*. Ann Arbor, MI: Servant, 1989.

—. *The Catholic Church and the Bible*. San Francisco: Ignatius, 1987.

Sungenis, Robert. *Not By Bread Alone*. Goleta, CA: Queenship, 2000.

Today's Missal, Easter/Pentecost. Portland: Oregon Catholic, 1997.

Twigg-Porter, George, S.J. *We Prepare for Mass*. Santa Barbara: Queenship.

Vianney, John. *The Little Catechism of The Cure of Ars*. Rockford, IL: Tan, 1951.

Wathen, Ambrose, O.S.B. *Silence*. Washington D.C.: Consortium, 1973.

Willimon, William H. *Word, Water, Wine, and Bread*. Valley Forge, PA: Judson, 1980.

1745648

Made in the USA